The Foreign
Businessman's Guide
to Doing Business
in Thailand

## ROBERT COOPER

*— By the author of Culture Shock Thailand —*

TIMES BOOKS INTERNATIONAL
*Singapore • Kuala Lumpur*

Feb: '92

to Nu, Tin Tin & Tessy

Published by Times Books International, an imprint
of Times Editions Pte Ltd

© Times Editions Pte Ltd
Times Centre
1 New Industrial Road
Singapore 1953

2nd Floor Wisma Hong Leong Yamaha
50 Jalan Penchala
46050 Petaling Jaya
Selangor Darul Ehsan
Malaysia

All rights reserved. No part of this publication may be
reproduced, stored in a retrieval system, or transmitted,
in any form or by any means, electronic, mechanical,
photo-copying, recording or otherwise, without the
prior permission of the copyright holder.

Set in Caslon540
Printed by Jin Jin Printing Industry Pte. Ltd.

ISBN 981 204 209 1

Before you read this book please consult your Managing Director if you suffer from a strong pathological need to believe in universal absolutes or obselete modern theories of absolute universals.

If you happen to be the Managing Director: this book will not demonstrate techniques for picking up a continent or even a small island for a string of beads. But it will give a hint of what can be had or lost for as little as a smile. A smile which, in Thailand at least, cannot with profit be delegated.

If you are a 9–9 manager, or if you think yourself a one minute manager, or if you don't know what these are or what you are, this book is especially for you, and my royalties. Thank you very much.

While all generalisations are tenuous, even this one, there are absolutely no universal absolutes, except for this one.

# A B C

The dogmatic *universals* of modern management
theories are not all relevant to business in Thailand.
Some are, some might be some of the time, some
will provide you with more problems than profit.

One thing leads to another, which leads on to other things
and sooner or later back to the beginning. The beginning
of most things is arbitrary and this is certainly true of the
world of business and the art, or skill, of management. All
components are interlinked and, whilst some are more
important than others, there is no essential or particularly
logical progression between the bits. This is my excuse for
setting out the little boxes of this book in the way they
come out of my filing index. ABC.

WHERE'S THE BEGINNING
AND WHERE'S THE END?

I THOUGHT
YOU'D TELL
ME

If further excuse is needed, let it be that this format is not only easiest to write, it is much easier to read and to flick through whilst standing in a bookshop trying to make up your mind if this book is just another how-to-manage-the-masses con job or a cost-effective tool to assist your management goals in Thailand.

I am also only too aware that comparatively few businessmen and managers read books and that even fewer have the time or inclination to start at the front and end at the back. So, if you happen to be reading this page before the rest, do feel completely at ease to stop right here and begin to flick pages in search of what interests you. To assist the busy flicker further, I have summarised the main points of each section briefly at the top, under the title.

Some among you will believe as I do that business and management are, to an extent that can affect profit margins and staff performance, culturally specific. No doubt you will, particularly in the enthusiasm which precedes arrival in the Land of Smiles and during that never ending settling in period following entry, want a base view of The Thais. This book does not contain everything you might want to know about Thai culture. For this you should buy and read the companion volume, *Culture Shock Thailand*, which is, to quote the Bangkok Post, not only "a thoroughly enjoyable book on Thai culture" but also "a must for anyone just arriving in the country as well as for the long term resident".

These pages call into question the dogmatic *universals* of modern management theories. Such widely-read and oft-repeated supposedly universal generalisations have been induced from the particular experiences of industrialisation in the West and, to a much lesser extent, in Japan, and are not all relevant to business in Thailand. Some are, some might be some of the time, some will provide the expat manager or businessman, with more problems than profit. Most attention is given to this last category: to pointing out where Thais at work differ from non-Thais, in terms perhaps of degree rather than absolute, but a degree significant enough to qualify the application of modern management methods, born in the West, to Thailand.

Sometimes, not too often and not too inappropriately I hope, I resort to generalisations and hoist myself on my own petard. Sometimes also I make light of the deadly serious. Never mind, as any and every Thai would say. If you can handle the small amount of contradiction and seeming flippancy contained in this book without too much trouble, there is a reasonable chance that you will survive, profit from and enjoy the Thai business world.

# ASSASSINATION

> The practice of assassination stands as evidence
> both of the importance and fragility of trust in
> business and of the reality that not every problem
> can be solved by face to face bargaining over
> the table.

Business, like diplomacy and marriage, is war by other
means. Things trundle along nicely as long as there is
mutual gain or exploitation and a willingness to compromise
based on trust. Trust of some sort is essential. It is built up
over time and like all things contains the seeds of its own
destruction. Trust can grow to fruition over years or
generations and vanish quicker than you can say "Et tu
Brutus?"

When trust flies out the window and all appears about to be lost in the winds of suspicion, hostility and violence, you always have the options of suicide or assassination. The Japanese, who otherwise demonstrate excellent business acumen, seem, in contemporary times, to have a penchant for the former. The Thai, like most other Asians, if faced with the choice, is more likely to plump for a rubbing out.

Knocking somebody out for keeps is not to be contemplated lightly. That would be immoral. It is not done, therefore, to leave such things until the last moment. The astute man of affairs will make his contingency plans at an early stage in a developing business relationship. Probably when shaking hands over the wet ink on the first contract in what promises, at the time, to be a long and mutually profitable relationship. Such just-in-case planning, whilst the champagne is still bubbling into the glass, is amoral and logical. Like the nuclear deterrent, it is only there to give you a chance, if it comes to it, to nuke first rather than last.

Given the choice between suicide and assassination, the reader with a basic grasp of economics and without an exceptionally generous and liberal insurance policy will readily appreciate the cost benefits of making a killing. At a stroke it removes the major source of competition and carries a good chance of improved fortune. It is, in Thailand, much cheaper than in the more industrialised countries, and it leaves the cleaning up to people other than your beloved family and friends.

The act of assassination has simple but important ground

rules. Do it as quickly as possible after realising that your trust has been broken. Never, ever, do it yourself. No matter how much you hate the bastard. And if more than one bastard is to be removed, do all of your killings at once: they will be sooner forgotten and there will be nobody around to get back at you.

The deed itself follows a well proven if somewhat unimaginative formula. A hired gunman from the beautiful town of Petburi draws up on a motorcycle alongside the target's traffic-bound Benz. At that precise time you are alibied up to the hairtips at the sixtieth birthday party of the most influential person you know.

The inevitable dark glass of the windows on the Benz often poses a small problem to the hitman, himself comporting the blackest pair of shades, thoughtfully mirrored on the outside to give the victim a final view of himself. This view should, unless your competitor has already commanded his own man from Petburi to wait for *your* Benz to leave the birthday party, be one of surprise. The professional dispatch rider will be used to such minor inconveniences as dingy vision and will have coolly pulled his gun from his shirt at the very moment the lights change to green and sprayed everybody in the car, just to make sure. The small drama will be marked only by a honking from behind and, perhaps, a paragraph two days later in the paper.

Let us offer an assurance to the expat entrepreneur that he is most unlikely, during his two or three years in Thailand, to become important enough to rub out. On the other hand, accidents can happen and the man from Petburi can hardly be expected to make an exception for you if you happen to be snuggled cheek by jowl with the man of the moment in the back of his Benz.

The practice of assassination is universally ignored by guides to sharpening business skills and modern management theory. It is however alive and thriving in many parts of the world, including Thailand, and stands as evidence of the importance and fragility of trust in business and the reality that not every problem can be solved by face to face bargaining over the table.

Assassination is not recommended for daily management of personnel. Neither is it very sporting to spring it on the visiting big sh*t from HQ who has kept you out of a director's chair for so many years.

One last small word on the subject. Like tax evasion and fiddling expenses, killing people for purely profit motives is against the law.

# BANGKOK AND BEYOND

You might be surprised to find that a Thai with
the prospect of moving to a far corner of Thailand
will, as you did before leaving home, ask himself
how he will cope with the local language, people
and food.

Bangkok is one of the few capitals in the world that
possesses a spoken opposite. The opposite of Bangkok is
"upcountry", which begins at that very vague and transient
point where Bangkok ends. Upcountry is a place
Bangkokians like to visit from time to time and the place
to send young people of dubious social merit, or older

people who hitch up too closely to the wrong patron.

All roads, rivers, railways and career opportunities lead to Bangkok. Which perhaps explains why the place is such a mess.

In spite of some lip service about decentralisation, Bangkok is still very much the place where things happen. Whether they are correct or not, most Thais have the idea that anything important gets done in the capital city and that a job in the centre of the world is more important than a job in the wilderness.

This view has been evident for several hundred years and is not likely to change overnight. It started when the capital was not Bangkok at all and the borders of the nation state were subject to fission and fusion. In such a situation the centrally located ruler of the Kingdom found it useful to invite all provincial chiefs and rulers of subject principalities to live in the royal palace. Maids, wives and concubines were included in the invitation but not armies. They were treated well and given tall pointed hats. They got to see fancy visiting embassies and lived at the trading heart of the Kingdom, where Chinese, Persians, Portuguese, English, Dutch and French competed for Thai patronage. Some were given jobs to do and symbols of rank and favour but none were provided with salaries.

These guests, under a divine ruler's gaze, clubbed together in intrigue groups to pass the time. Such intrigues could be successful and lead to the advancement of a clique or they could fail and lead to torture and death. The stakes for foreign businessmen of the period, who could not help but fall in with the system if they were to steal an advantage over their competitors, were often equally high. Some amassed fortunes and fled the scene. Others lost their heads in the capital city.

The pull of the capital remains strong. People move into not out of Bangkok. When you set up a sub-office in Hang Dong, think very carefully about staffing. It might just be that one of your Bangkok-based staff is not only suitable for the job but comes from there and would actually not mind going back. If on the other hand the person you have in mind as sub-office head has a strong aversion to living upcountry, even if it means promotion, better think again.

Try to remember that the person will be considering many of the same factors that troubled your mind before leaving home: what about my family? should I take the children or leave them with Auntie so they can continue at the same school? should I take my wife/husband, and what about her/his career? what are the medical services like? Do not presume that just because a person is Thai, he or she will be happy to move anywhere within the Kingdom. Relatives and friends and the social life of a large office are important considerations to anybody, particularly a Thai.

You might also be surprised to find that a Thai with the prospect of moving to a far corner of the land will, as you did, ask himself how he will cope with the local language, people and food. Yes, the people. Not only does Thailand have at least four distinct dialects of Thai, with matching cuisines and other cultural differences, it is also very much divided into educated and comparatively uneducated people. You might be charmed by the rustic rice farmers, but your university educated sub-office head might feel very lonely in their company.

Last but not at all least in the Thai mind will be evaluation of status implied in the move. A small promotion and a little more money will not compensate for receiving orders from the Bangkok office signed by an inferior. Surprisingly, this happens all the time. A sensible expat manager will boost sub-office morale whenever possible. You stay in contact with the sub-office, at least by signing communications, and the people out there can let themselves believe that you are noting their efforts even more than you did when they were in the office next door. Praise especially takes on an added significance when it is signed by the boss, and preferably copied all over the status hierarchy. And it doesn't cost you anything.

# BIG MEN

When you are long gone, the system will still
be there.

The occasional glib generalisation about the nature of
Thais and the society they have formed for themselves is
necessary if you are to understand, in the shortest time,
with the minimum of effort, and of course the maximum
of profit, how the business environment in Thailand differs
from the one in which you earned or otherwise acquired
your officer's stripes. Such a proposition is that all of Thai
society is divided into big people and little people.

Do not confuse with simple class society. Even the

biggest people behave like little people when interacting with royalty and when faced with any monk. Big and little are comparative concepts. There is always somebody bigger and there is always somebody smaller. There are also ways to become bigger without throwing the world into bloody social revolution. It is basically all rather individual. The big mix with the big, each knowing his place while trying to get bigger all the time, and the littlest sit with others of their kind. Five hundred or so families might be considered firmly ensconced in the big people bracket, but group solidarity is far short of forming a social class in the Western sense.

Thai language doesn't bother very much with distinguishing between the sexes. Thus, big people and little people are terms literally translated from Thai. Thais use these terms all the time. In reality, big *men* are the important human animals of which to beware and to which to toady. Big women exist in their own right in fairly small numbers but as a reflection of the power of their men in droves.

You should not even think of joining the ranks of the really big. These are riddled with intrigue, alliances and clique loyalties and betrayals. Insinuate with caution: you are walking on a bamboo pole across a quicksand. For every friend you might think you make, there is at least one new enemy unknown to you. For the first twenty years or so, concentrate simply on avoiding offence.

With a few notable exceptions, who are usually so old they are more interested in accumulating religious merit for the next life rather than profit for this one and who might appear sincerely friendly and helpful to an expat lost in the maze, big men are recognisable by their appalling behaviour.

When surrounded by little people, the big man is prone to gross lapses of social etiquette. He will take social norm reversal to the brink, but not over the brink. The *wai* of lesser mortals are ignored or recognised by being waved aside. A wretched subordinate is asked a question and his reply cut short, ignored or disagreed with. When you see this happen, hopefully to somebody other than you, observe the little man. If he can bring himself to say another word, it will certainly not be a defence of his original statement but an ingratiating apology for his stupidity and a crawling eulogy to the superior reasoning of the big man.

The rules for dealing with a big man are simple enough. Stay behind him when walking and below him whenever physically possible. Talk only when invited and never contradict. Agree even when the big man makes the most awful mistakes and never, ever point out that he is contradicting himself with every sentence.

Bowing to ill-informed authority and meeting social abuse by singing the praises of your abuser will encourage the big man to like you. If indeed he notices that you are there at all. All this is completely alien to modern management theory and almost guaranteed to make any business consultant sounding out the country take the first plane back to Zurich.

It is most important, to any expat manager, to understand why Thais behave in such a subservient way in front of men who have power. It has everything to do with the traditional system of career advancement, which is based on patronage. Subordinates who follow the leader are rewarded: those who do not are got rid of. Not so very different in essence to what really goes on in the management of any company anywhere. Certainly more obvious in Thailand and perhaps more honest. At least people know the system and their place in it. It is a system built up over centuries and unlikely to change much for a very long time. You must come to terms with it and realize that it contains many real advantages that more than balance the occasional humbling before a bigger man than you.

As a manager or boss, you are a big man to your subordinate. His or her behaviour will be qualified by his knowledge of foreigners and the fact that your patronage is limited to what he can reasonably expect to get out of you during the term of your stay. Certainly you will not be looking after him for the rest of his life. If he keeps his nose clean and does not get on your wrong side, he can expect a reasonable performance evaluation report and, perhaps, a recommendation for or granting of promotion.

One or two underlings might, in an attempt to please you and advance themselves in your eyes, have read some awful book on "effective management" and feel that they are expected to demonstrate initiative by disagreeing with everything you say. Most will, however, treat you politely and with a respect you never had back home. By all means enjoy it. But do not react big man style. There is no excuse for abuse and anyway you lack the real power base to make or break people, so don't pretend you have it. Try not to buck the system too much. After all, when you are long gone the system will still be there.

Be friendly by all means, but without being friends. Take care of your people, at least those who work *and* accord you status, and you are half way there.

# BLESSING

Can you really trust anybody who has not renounced your world to bless you and hope that you will be richer than they?

If you are starting up business in Thailand, you certainly will need all the help you can get. Thus, once you have located premises and staff, waste no time in obtaining the monks' blessing on your enterprise.

Monks are so far away from the profit motive that they have renounced grasping after life itself and exist only from day to day on whatever is placed in their bowls.

These are the perfect beings to bless your overheads and the future prosperity of your business venture.

If there is any paradox involved in this, don't worry about it. The paradox is in your mind, not in the minds of your Buddhist staff. The great respect in which the monks and their way of life are held by your staff in no way indicates subversive tendencies towards renunciation of profit by the very people you are counting on to realise it. On the contrary, it indicates a very realistic understanding of the competitive nature of the business world. Can you really trust those who have not renounced your world to bless you and hope that you will be richer than they?

Whatever your views on the likely effect on profits of feeding nine monks, listening to them chant in Pali from scriptures written long before the Holy Roman Empire and witnessing a daubing of dots over your doors, rest assured that you are making a sound economic investment.

The cost-effectiveness of the morning may be a little difficult for the corporeal bodies back in Headquarters to grasp fully, especially if you have not had the good sense to send them a dozen copies of this book. Never mind. Immediate gains are: a happy workforce, increased status for you, and your clear demonstration that you are quite prepared to do things the Thai way when the goal is the welfare of your people and business. Symbolically, the ceremony "networks" your business affairs with the collective social life of your workforce and the most important of Thai institutions, the Buddhist order of monks known as the Sangha. It also ensures that when things do go wrong later in your venture, your local staff will not blame you for skimping on the opening.

Somebody among your staff will know all that has to be done for the ceremony. If you happen to have only a small office staffed by young people who are not sure of protocol, one of them will know someone older and wiser to invite in for the occasion as adviser. All you have to do, in addition to providing money for food, is to ensure transport for the abbot and eight other monks who will come to your premises at an agreed time in the morning. Usually they will stay about two hours and leave soon after midday. They must finish eating before noon. Once they have blessed the premises, sprinkled water around and been respectfully seen to the cars which will take them back to the temple, everybody can eat the leftovers, which of course are deliberately substantial. To eat the leftovers of monks is considered to bring good luck, as well as good food, so allow plenty to eat and plenty of time for a lucky lunch.

As the main sponsor of the ceremony, you will take a prominent role. Not of course as prominent as any of the monks. Don't whatever you do try to upstage the monks. Being humble and respectful before your infinite superiors is the rule, which in turn will gain you the respect of your subordinates. As Number One you will be first in line to welcome the monks with a *wai*. When the time comes to serve the food, you get first go. If the rice is to be spooned out, give just a little to each monk, starting with the abbot and working away from him, i.e. down the line of status. Giving a little in these circumstances is not a sign of meanness but of generosity. Instead of grabbing all the merit for yourself, you leave the opportunity for your staff to make merit by following along behind you, in their own order of status, until the many plates set in front of the monks are full.

Before the monks get up to leave, it is customary to give each a package containing soap, razor blades, mosquito coils and similar small utilitarian items of daily use. You will also show your appreciation by again going on your knees before the monks, abbot first of course, and respectfully handing over individual envelopes containing a generous amount of money for the abbot and reasonably generous amounts of money for the other monks. Don't be surprised. I thought we had agreed, or I had told you, a few paragraphs ago, that any paradox is all in your mind.

If you happen to be one of those rarities, a woman boss, then receiving blessings is yet another activity that is going to be a lot harder for you than for a man. You cannot touch monks or their robes and you cannot pass anything directly to a monk; you place offerings on a special cloth that the monk will set out before him or you go through an intermediate man. But don't be put off by a few difficulties. Once the monks realise that it really is a woman throwing the party, they are likely to revel in the novelty. And while it is true that all monks are men, it is equally true that the monkhood survives because of women, who offer food on the morning alms round and convince their sons to take on robes. At one throw of the dice you demonstrate that you know how to behave correctly as a humble woman and that you are the boss. And no talk of paradoxes.

Whether you are man or woman, the blessing will leave

you with a warm glow and some nice photos. The warm glow you get might come from the blessing or it might come from the obvious appreciation your Thai staff will feel for a foreigner who respects what they respect, or at least behaves as if he does. Take it as a sign that you have started right.

# BOREDOM

In Thailand, the highest goal of life is achieved not through hard work but by sitting quietly doing nothing.

*When a man is without work he is bored.* So reads our Guide to Effective Management. Idle hands do the devil's work. Freedom through work. Joy through work. Man creates himself through work. Endless cliches spawned by an obscure Protestant Ethic which so cruelly assumed reality in a twentieth century dominated by conflicting Western political ideologies, each of which claims universal truth for its doctrine. In much the same way, contemporary business management theory assumes eternal and monolithic application of its dogma. Thus has the eulogy of work spread in epidemic proportions to all nations. Who would deny that work is central to human dignity? Isn't it in a UN Charter somewhere? Then it must be true. Man can work his way to heaven and/or work his way to paradise on earth. Isn't that glorious? Take away work and stupid man knows not what to do with himself.

Well folks, it is all a lie. I know because I would rather play or do nothing than work. And so would most Thais. In Thailand the highest goal of life, complete detachment, is achieved not through hard work but by sitting quietly doing nothing.

The face of the old hawker sitting at the roadside all day beside the Bangkok traffic carries the same quiet resignation as that of the monk sitting quietly in a village temple. Whatever few baht fate directs towards the hawker will be received. Whatever food is placed in the monk's bowl he will eat. The long hours sitting quietly are no cause for frustration, mischief or boredom.

Most Thais can sit and wait much more happily than most expat managers. Views on boredom are not the same. The Thai worker will say he is "bored" if his work is unpleasant or solitary or even too demanding. If he or she has nice surroundings and opportunities for chit-chat, he or she will work steadily and happily enough.

Do not tie yourself up in knots seeking to enrich jobs through diversification, participation or rotation or whatever. You will be much more popular if you can bring yourself to leave people alone as far as is reasonably

possible. If you must interfere, ask yourself why. Could it be an unhealthy obsession with work for work's sake? Or is it perhaps that *you* are bored? Why not try sitting quietly doing nothing? For many a Thai this is the starting point. And a logical one it is too. If you can't even learn to do nothing properly, how on earth are you ever going to learn to do something?

# CHINESE

Knowledge of Chinese dialects and of the important Thais who use these dialects might or might not be important to your business objectives. If such knowledge is important, you must have it on your side.

To distinguish Thai-Chinese from Thai-Thai is easy. You have only to ask. The Chinese are the ones who reply that they are 100% Thai. And they are. At the same time, quite a few, particularly those in the world of business and commerce, are 100% Chinese.

Chinese traders and settlers were enjoying harmonious and mutually beneficial relations with Thais long before the seventeenth century incursions into Thailand of contending European factions, who came first as fortune seeking adventurers, then as monopoly minded trading companies, then as glorious travelling embassies, then as convert-hungry missionaries and finally as would be colonizers complete with gunboats and musketeers.

Initially, there was no conflict between Europeans, Thais and Chinese and some useful mutual gains to be had by all. Europe had few trade goods of much interest to Asia apart from superior armaments. But it did open up new markets for raw materials, silks, tea, spices, porcelain, hides and ivory, which originated in Thailand, China or

Japan. These were available through Chinese middle men in the old Thai capital of Ayudhya, at the time one of Asia's most important centres of trade.

While the Chinese were happy to live in Thailand and work without aspirations other than increasing trade and profit, the Europeans brought their national conflicts with them onto Thai soil. The end result was not too long in coming. After brief romances with Portugal, the Netherlands, England and France, Thailand had the very good sense to realise that small matters such as extra-territorial rights and the armed forts cropping up in little known places such as Bangkok could well be the thin edge of an unwanted wedge. Thus, the Europeans were all invited to leave and, after a few exchanges of gunfire and hostages, duly left to colonize the rest of Southeast Asia.

As the Europeans were packing their trunks, the Chinese were going about business as usual. After a long time Europeans were welcomed back as traders but never again seriously attempted to colonize the Kingdom. Thus Thailand remained the only Southeast Asian country to avoid political domination by a Western power.

The colonial presence in the rest of Southeast Asia had a strong tendency to segregate Chinese settlers from the indigenous populations. This was not the case in Thailand. Tolerance and mutual gain on both sides, together with significant cultural similarities and a Chinese willingness to adopt Thai ways, at least in public, assisted community interaction. Intermarriage bred integration and led finally to a continuing process of assimilation. This is the reason why many Thais have no difficulty at all in seeing themselves as 100% Thai *and* as Chinese.

There is a popular, if less than accurate, view of Thais of Chinese origin as controllers of the stock market and the business world, cloistered in Bangkok's China Town from which they make forays into mining and sugar plantations. While their presence is most noticeable in the Chinese character of China Town's shophouses, most Thai-Chinese are spread throughout the smaller towns of Thailand and many pursue agricultural activities in villages and homesteads in the remotest parts of the country.

To ask what proportion of the Thai population is *Chinese* is pointless. Some people maintain Chinese religious practices in addition to Thai Buddhism or Christianity and some use a Chinese name and speak a Chinese dialect at home. Many others have not a single cultural characteristic which is not Thai, but look Chinese. It is very difficult, if not impossible, to find a Thai-Chinese who does not have some Thai ancestry and almost as difficult to find a Thai with no percentage of Chinese in him. Thus the question of what is Thai and what is Chinese is likely to be of more interest to the anthropologist than to the business manager.

Even if and when you discover that your Thai staff is largely Chinese, you will not need to adjust your behaviour since Thai norms predominate. Do not expect the "Thai-Chinese", born and educated in Thailand, to behave like his distant ethnic cousin in Hong Kong or Beijing. Be aware, however, that links of dialect and clan remain important among Bangkok's business elite. Do not be surprised to find Thais at your business meetings exchanging confidences in Teo Chew or another dialect. Knowledge of Chinese dialects and of the important Thais who use those dialects might or might not be important to your business objectives. If such knowledge is important, you must have it on your side. You cannot personally learn even one dialect and even if you did you would still be excluded from the club, but if your comprador has at least one foot in the dialect door so much the better for you.

# COMMUNICATION

The expat business manager in Thailand can increase his performance and his company's profits by being sensitive to the particularly Thai nature of communication between people in Thailand.

Communication between people is essential to running any business anywhere in the world. Communication is also essential to the maintenance of any culture anywhere in the world. And since all cultures differ to a greater or lesser extent from all other cultures, otherwise they would cease to exist, it seems reasonable enough, at least to me, to suspect that forms of communication and the messages being passed back and forth within different cultures are not universal. In so far as businesses, even multinational ones, have the base or bases of their profit in a particular culture, or in several different particular cultures, profitable communications logically relate to the existing norms of communication within the culture(s) of the people producing the profit.

In Thailand the message is very closely related to the form of communication. This is as true for the spoken or written forms, with which you might think you are reasonably experienced, as it is for a smile, frown, keep-them-guessing mask of indifference, and a multitude of forms of body language which might be new to you. The message conveyed by the form is respect, subservience, superiority, arrogance, anger or fear, equality, friendship, dislike, pleasure or displeasure. All this before you get down to actual content, which for you might be of primary importance but for the Thai recipient of your message could be secondary. Once you have offended somebody by your tone of voice, by a letter that you considered friendly but the recipient finds insulting, by a well intended suggestion for improvements that is taken as a criticism, or even by a give-away frown when a smile would be appropriate, don't expect him to be so very interested in analysing the content of your message or receptive to doing what you want of him.

Shared or translated symbols of communication are needed if you are to get the message from your brain to the minds of the bodies paid to do the work. Your thoughts, opinions and orders might leave your lips and pen, but unless they are picked up and acted upon they remain in effect ideas in your head. If they stay in your head they are useless. If there is no communication, there is no management.

# COMPETITION

Competition, in spite of the superficially free-wheeling capitalism that seems to characterise the Thai business world, is a word and action to be avoided. There is no such thing as friendly competition.

*Fair competition* is something of a contradiction in terms in the business world of any country. It is yet to be established as the norm in Thailand.

Nobody anywhere likes to lose. In Thailand, nobody has to. Thais are expert at arranging the kind of elaborate and ritualistic competition which demonstrates symbiotic opposition. A contest where both sides gain, where everybody has a good time, and where similarities are more evident than differences.

Some "competing" towns and provinces, trading posts on opposite banks of Thailand's major waterways and on the Mekhong river between Thailand and its ethnic brother Laos, have been taking part in boat races for much longer than Oxford and Cambridge. Unlike the Oxbridge annual race, the Thais do not go in for a single win or lose event. Instead there will be a long series of races. Each will have a winner, but at the end of the day it is often impossible to say who won. This is exactly how it should be, with neither side controlling an absolute advantage.

Towns and villages often come together in good natured competition between social groups, most often those formed by different temple communities. Some of these competitions have now developed into tourist attractions: the candle festival in Ubon, where temple communities compete to carve the most beautiful giant candle at the beginning of Buddhist Lent; the Loy Khratong festival in Chiang Mai, when floats constructed by temple groups or sponsored by commercial enterprises are paraded through the streets, and the many Miss Songkran contests that take place everywhere during Thai New Year. Most competitive events, however, remain simple occasions for coming together to have fun, where taking part is more important than doing one's best in order to win, and where there is no deliberate attempt to make your competitor lose.

Unfortunately, the spirit of playing the game is, in this day and age, sometimes unwittingly or wittingly replaced with the urge to win. All right perhaps when Thai boxing or cock-fighting is involved but not so good when a contest involves people or parties who have to work together and must be on good terms.

Please excuse me dear reader while I step out of style to illustrate this last point by telling you a parable with a moral which might just persuade you that aggressive competitive urges are not always in the interests of the best man, if by chance he should win. It won't take long.

Not so long ago I was invited to the annual pre-harvest sports day between two neighbouring villages. I expected the usual sequence of opening parade, speeches by local big men, and a sharing of prizes throughout the day between the two sides. From the first moment however things began to go wrong. After both sides stood together for the national anthem, competition became cut throat.

One side put on its usual parade. Farmers young and not so young marched past in odds and ends sports clothes; uniformly out of step but never mind. The other side, sporting spotless mock Adidas jogging suits, stepped out in harmony to the carefully orchestrated music of its well practised band and staggered the two-village audience by displays of gymnastics from its schoolchildren. The same side went on to win almost all of the prizes. As the day wore on, the inevitable drinking groups formed and far from the usual jesting that accompanies a drinking bout (at least at the beginning), villagers from the losing side began to insult the winners and to accuse them of cheating, taking stimulants and bribing the judges. Very quickly things became ugly and the final events were abandoned as fights broke out. The local police at first tried to keep order but failed because most had loyalties to one side or the other. Finally a nearby army school sent its trainee officers to break things up. Ten villagers were hospitalised, one with a serious gunshot wound.

The sports day failed to confirm good relations between two villages which shared the cost and labour involved in repairs on a common road to market and depended on cooperation in the maintenance and use of a single water source to irrigate the rice fields of both sides. Instead the opposite result was achieved and the management of mutual economic benefits suffered because social relations had been soured by aggressive competition. Village elders were left with a lot of work to do to repair relations, which remained cool until the following year's sports day in which there were no acrobatics and mediocrity of performance ensured a fair distribution of wins between the two sides.

The reason for the anomalous sports day was not hard to find. The winning village had newly acquired an enthusiastic sports freak as schoolmaster. No doubt with the best of intentions he began serious training during the school months before the big day and encouraged villagers to come to the school for training by introducing a series of competitive knockout contests to select the most physically able to take part in the inter-village meet. He certainly developed a fine *esprit de corps* among those villagers selected to represent their village but failed to understand the real objective of the event and therefore made the mistake of training them to win rather than to break even. And that is the moral of the story. Better not to play at all than to play to win or lose.

In the urban workplace, as in the village, it is not good sportsmanship to outshine your fellows by performing better than them. Many an expat manager has been taken by surprise when the person on his staff whom he has selected as the most competent, and has sent off for courses to improve communication skills and administrative expertise, is rejected by his colleagues or refuses a promotion that would set him above and apart.

At the supra-enterprise level, when tempted to go for more than your share, enter open competition at your peril and in the knowledge that you are almost sure to lose. There is no way any but the biggest of foreign enterprises, which usually have a near monopoly on the product, produce or service, or go in for export only, will develop or purchase the support of enough sufficiently influential persons to permit swallowing up the smaller fish and openly taking on the sharks. On the other hand, if you base your business relationships on mutual gains and are content to do somewhat better than break even, you might find that your Thai business associates will help you out when you need them.

Competition, in spite of the superficially free-wheeling capitalism that seems to characterise the Thai business world, is a word and action to be avoided. Don't talk of friendly competition, only friendly cooperation.

# COMPLAINTS

Being nice helps people like you and builds the kind of long term obligation to provide service which just does not follow from blasting an unseen ear over the telephone.

When the photocopy machine breaks down for the third time in a month and the renting agency takes a week to send a mechanic. When the brand label falls off the new computer followed by various other parts. When your office car comes back from service with an extra thousand kilometres on the clock. When the plumber repairs a leaky water pipe with sticky tape and elastic bands. Then you begin to feel that you are being had. And you probably are. So much for Thai sensitivities and the criticism taboo. If these things happen anywhere in the world, complaints are in order.

In circumstances like these it is not easy, and not always appropriate, to be polite, friendly and private. But if you can be, it might pay in the long run. Being nice helps people like you and builds the kind of long term obligation to provide service which just does not follow from blasting somebody's unseen ear over the telephone. If people get to like you, there is more of a likelihood that they will do things to help you, or knock something or everything off your bill, or do it right and quicker next time.

There are, of course, limits to being nice. Thailand may teach you yours.

# COMPRADOR

You are interested in the shortest route to efficient and profitable operations and management. Your comprador should be able to show you the way.

In addition to managing your staff, you will, to a varying degree depending on the nature of your business, need to be in touch with Thai business contacts, government officials, and influential people. You will need to build alliances and know your enemies, or potential enemies, and how to neutralise them. You will need an information system which amounts to a genteel spy network. In all of this, you will certainly need some capable and well placed assistance.

Since the seventeenth century, all of the earlier foreign business enterprises in Thailand have felt the same need. The successful survived because they worked through a Thai *comprador*, a person of influence who owed his loyalty to Thailand but who received money from foreigners in exchange for his assistance in promoting the foreigners' objectives. A comprador held an important and respected position.

The term comprador is still in use in English and in Thai. In English it now has pejorative connotations related to the spread of European imperialism. In Thai also it has lost its original meaning and usually now refers to a financial broker (without any pejorative undercurrents). Although use of the term had best be avoided in communications with HQ, the foreign entrepreneur or manager will certainly need a modern comprador of some sort if he is to survive and prosper. Call him or her what you will, partner, adviser, deputy, assistant, consultant, or even secretary. But know that an efficient comprador is necessary to effective operations.

The role, power and recompense of the comprador will vary according to the reasons he is employed. However, even those foreigners who have established successful small enterprises in the Kingdom entirely through their own efforts need a Thai partner. Such a foreigner might have lived in the country most of his life, speak fluent Thai, and be accepted by Thais as Thai. He could even have a national reputation and access to the highest of social circles. He thinks Thai. And because of this, he plays it safe.

Your comprador should be something of a magician. Day to day bureaucratic problems, which can stifle your company and you, will disappear. When you come to the table to sign contracts, it will be for symbolic discussion, probably some last minute light-hearted ritual of bargaining and commemorative photographs. All of the work and magic has been done behind the scenes but not behind your back by your comprador and the person in the other camp with whom he or she most probably went to school. Problems of project implementation, import and export regulations, building permits and so on: your comprador is there to smooth things over.

Your modern version comprador will owe loyalty to you as well as the company. Most likely he or she has really been running the Thailand part of the empire for years already and you have only to fit in and make yourself liked. If such arrangements already exist, count your blessings. Disrupt them at your peril.

If you find yourself replacing a failed manager, it may be because nobody is performing the comprador's role. Lose no time in correcting the situation. Look carefully around your staff. They were probably recruited because of high education and proficiency in English, qualities which are becoming increasingly available but are still very much valued. Not so long ago a really well-educated Thai was rare enough that he or she was likely to know personally many of the like educated (and well placed) and to be related to at least some.

Do not immediately jump at the person who speaks English well and with whom you get on easily. Getting on well with a foreigner does not necessarily mean getting on as well with important Thais. Pay particular attention to the middle-aged and those who already have a position of respect and leadership among your staff. Remember that you will, to a greater or lesser extent, be taking your chosen one out of the womb of his or her social group. Both the individual and the group could become unhappy and less productive. The last thing you want is to create jealousy and conflict. If there is any risk of doing so, it is probably better to look elsewhere.

Decide as quickly as you can if you simply need someone who knows his way around customs procedures or if you are flying much higher. A comprador with court connections is not a must if you are managing a restaurant on Patpong. An ex-policeman could be helpful.

As you already know, the most important decisions of all involve picking the people who will do the work for you. And selecting an appropriate comprador is likely to be the most important placement decision you make during your career in Thailand. Certainly you will give the decision your time and thought.

If there is no clear inside candidate for the role, you will have to recruit. Be careful. Employ a Thai *only* because of good social contacts and he could turn out to be inefficient, dishonest and very hard to get rid of. The surest way to get the reasonably sure assistance of a good comprador is to poach a known good one from another foreign company, which is not easy and will certainly involve offering much more money and non-taxable incentives.

# CONFLICT

To ignore the real and pragmatic reasons why Thais are so keen on the maintenance of harmony is, for the manager, to fail to capitalise on one of the most attractive attributes of Thai ethics.

Open conflict and violence are seen by Thais as the effect of unsuppressed human anger. The way to avoid conflict is to avoid anger by taking a Buddhist middle path between extremes and by detachment, the cultivation of neutral feelings between love and hate.

In the workplace, you might not immediately appreciate the benefits of this studied non-involvement and neutralism. You might even tend to dismiss it as a negative characteristic. To do so is to ignore the real and practical reasons why Thais are keen on the maintenance of harmony. For the manager, it also fails to capitalise on one of the most attractive attributes of Thai ethics.

To understand the economic base for the ethic of conflict avoidance, you have only to look outside of your urban work environment to the agricultural communities in which most Thais continue to live and work. In such communities differences of wealth and status exist but the economic welfare and social prestige of individual families depends on the maintenance of harmony within the group. Conflict disrupts patterns of mutual help in such important activities as the construction and maintenance of irrigation systems, flood control, roads and the many activities associated with rice cultivation. Conflict also reduces a community's ability to defend itself: in the not so distant old days against thieves and bandits and these days against land developers and speculators.

Moving from the comparative security of the agricultural community to the comparative insecurity of the town does not overnight change an individual's coping mechanisms, particularly when no alternative ways of avoiding urban violence are on offer. If anything, urbanisation has increased Thai inclination towards conflict avoidance, which remains very evident even in the anarchy of Bangkok. The consensus of village society is lacking, but the man who keeps cool and steers clear of trouble not only stays alive but also earns the respect of his friends and workmates.

As your exposure to Thai ways of doing things increases, so you are likely to develop more respect for those members of your staff who are clearly practised in the art of avoiding trouble. One steady worker who perhaps does not stand out in terms of dynamism and initiative and shows no great interest in taking over his supervisor's job is a treasure to be valued and looked after. If everybody on your team seems to be that way, thank your lucky stars.

# CRAFTSMANSHIP

The craftsman approach produces nicely finished
products. Slow and sure and never mind the time.
It might take some reeducation, and careful
monitoring, to switch concentration onto quantity,
while maintaining a quality which is acceptable to
the continued maintenance of sales.

The combination of form and function in traditional
craftsmanship has produced the unique beauty of
Thailand's temples and houses, exquisitely woven and
embroidered cloth, silk and silverwork, basketwork,
decorated ox-carts and many functional items that fetch
high prices in Thailand's antique shops and overseas. Even
the block of wood to sit on while grating coconuts was
always carved into a beautiful rabbit or some other animal.

Pure function was never enough. The useful had to be
beautiful. Beautiful to the eyes of the craftsman and the
eyes of his neighbours, grandparents and grandchildren.
Beautiful according to the prevailing conception of
aesthetics in Thai society, in which, until recently, almost
everybody was a craftsman of some sort and now, it
suddenly seems, almost nobody is.

Things are changing fast in Thailand, as everywhere,
and, at least when it comes to craftsmanship, not necessarily
for the better. Fantasy has run rampant through the

49

construction industry, ideas on Western fashion have replaced Thai dress for daily wear, and even the coconut grating rabbit, until recently seen sitting under every Thai house, has been replaced by a cheap stick of wood with a grater on the end that has less aesthetic appeal than the average potato peeler in the West.

Traditional culture is still appreciated but craftsmanship has become largely the preserve of specialists, few of whom earn very much and most of whom are obliged to sell their products more expensively than the new mass-produced modern equivalents.

In one generation the Thais passed from a self-sufficient to a specialised-producer economy and society. In the current generation the mass-produced machine tool product has almost taken over. And why not? The same process of socio-economic change happened *long ago* in the industrial world. Which is perhaps the whole point.

Thailand, still an agricultural country, has gone through a great deal of change *very recently*. Today's worker on your shopfloor or in your office, even if, as is quite possible, he or she comes from an agricultural community in the north or northeast, is not likely to be much of a craftsman in the traditional sense. But something of a craftsman way of doing things lives on.

The craftsman approach produces nicely finished products, slow and sure and never mind the time. It might take some reeducation, and careful monitoring, to switch concentration onto quantity, while at the same time of course maintaining a quality which is acceptable to the continued maintenance of sales. Hurry your workers along on activities which are comparatively new to them and outside of any reference to known standards and you can watch the quality leak away like the water seeping through your fancy new plumbing. Onto the floor and down the drain.

# CRAWLING

Correct crawling is a cost effective way of manipulating people who have more power and authority than you. Don't underestimate it, particularly in Thailand. At the same time, it is of the utmost importance to know when to crawl, what to do, how far to go and when to stop.

Modern management manuals inevitably overlook or minimize or even advise against the widespread practice of bowing and scraping to achieve management and self-advancement objectives. By so doing they fail to make use of one of the most powerful means of influence available to the manager and show a less than satisfactory understanding of what people are really like and what they really like.

What they really like is for you, who seek their favour, to give a sign of deferential obeisance which makes it clear that you recognise a superior being when you have the luck to meet one.

Most top people everywhere respond to a bit of squirming and grovelling by liking you. Then when somebody mentions your name they are much more likely to allow that you are a competent person from a respectable company. It costs nothing except your self-esteem, which in Thailand is repaired as soon as some lesser mortals have cringingly kowtowed to you. Correct crawling is therefore a cost-effective way of manipulating people who have more power and authority than you. Don't underestimate it, particularly in Thailand. At the same time, it is of the utmost importance to know when to crawl, what to do, how far to go and, most important of all, when to stop.

The last thing you would want to do is to suck up to those who should rightly be sucking up to you. Thus, the first thing to do is to ascertain who is a bigger man than you are. This is often not immediately evident unless you have an anthropologist's eye for rites of inversion. Really big men can, if they feel like it, turn up in Adidas hat and sneakers and farmer's shirt when everybody else is uniformed up to look like admirals of the fleet. The best of preparations comes to nothing if you fail to recognise the fellow when he finally makes his overdue appearance. And of course to get in first before you are lost in a sea of grovel.

It is not at all good for your economic welfare to ignore the scruffy git attempting to hump his beer paunch out of the car and it is social suicide to compound the insult by crawling in front of his well-dressed chauffeur. Your comprador should fill you in. And being filled in, you might like to keep notes in your genteel spy network confidential file.

Do not worry too much at first with questions as to the very important person's usefulness to your objectives. Some of these guys have fingers in many more pies than you have pies or they have fingers. In any case, the basic crawling procedures are a big man's due and not negotiable. Later, when you feel more comfortable in your crawling, you can and *must* become more selective. At first, however, you can simply regard it all as practice of management techniques which are, even if you have yessed your way to where you are today, bound to feel a bit strange to you at first. Unless you happen to be Japanese.

Basic crawling requires the very best low *wai* on meeting and separating, asking permission if you really cannot wait to go outside to vomit or shoot yourself, not sitting until He has taken what He thinks is the best chair, not crossing your legs even if dying for a pee, not being higher or further forward than He, speaking quietly and only when spoken to, answering rather than questioning, avoiding controversy like the plague, and saying absolutely nothing smacking of self promotion or significance. Be a good little boy and perhaps Daddy might take care of you, or at least not make your life unbearable.

Just about everybody likes the attentions of an

accomplished crawler. But have care your fawning does not make a turn towards vulgarity. Learn fast how far you should go and, even if you have begun to discover a kinky pleasure in the art of prostration and boot licking, exercise self restraint before you become completely consumed. The climax of self-abasement is a very difficult act to follow should fortune shine and the Man throw you a sprat or a mackerel. So always keep a little something in reserve. Remember, it is dangerous to make your intentions transparently obvious and to stand out from the crowd too far. Even when on your knees.

# CREATIVITY

Don't complicate your life and your workers' lives by trying to make them happy, creative and productive.

*Everyone feels happy when he creates something altogether new, useful or beautiful.* A quotation from one of the multitude of books on modern management which preaches that happy workers are more creative and therefore contribute more to overall productivity. What the book's universal statement fails to say is that ideas on what constitutes new, useful and beautiful might not be at all the same for the worker and the manager. This is likely to be particularly the case if the worker is Thai and the manager is expatriate.

If your only goal is to keep your workers happy, all right. Let them play. But if you have the additional goal and quite possibly the priority goal of having your production workers and office staff do what *you* think is new, useful or beautiful, you are unlikely to find the advice in the quotation very helpful.

Never mind. There is every reason *not* to complicate your life and your workers' lives by trying to make them happy, productive *and* creative, which would undoubtedly mean *them* conforming to *your* ideas of creativity. Before you could say "effective management", you would most likely find the smiles disappearing down the drain along with quality and productivity.

No longer does the worker have the pleasure and pride of weaving her own dress or forging his own knife. That is not your fault. But there is no need to pretend that twisting off plastic things and packing them in a box or typing out your memos can serve as a fully satisfactory replacement activity. They cannot. Not even if you encourage your workers to design the packing boxes or allow your staff the additional burden of drafting your memos before you change them. Thais will do what the boss tells them to do, within reason and ability, and they will smile their way through but they neither want nor need your concept of creativity in order to get by. And there is really no good reason why you should want them to want it.

# CRITICISM

During your career in Thailand, it is safer and more productive to forget anything you might have come to believe about the value of constructive criticism and to be aware that any criticism is likely to have negative rather than positive effects.

In the West, it is admirable for two people to disagree in public, be critical of each other's ideas or methods in a meeting, agree to disagree or to reach a constructive compromise, remain friends, and go off for a drink together after work. Some modern managers do manage this extraordinary feat, although it very much depends on the shame threshold of both parties. Do not expect Thais to behave in this strange way.

In Thailand, open criticism is seen as a form of violence. It hurts people. It threatens superficial harmony. It disturbs the peace. It is negative. It is rarely, if ever, entered into with the idea of improving a situation, but is sometimes used as a weapon to destroy enemies. The act of criticism, depending on the directness and intensity with which it is delivered, is seen at best as a sign of bad manners and at worst as a deliberate attempt to offend, shame and destroy.

A Thai criticised by you in public is likely to give very little thought to whether the criticism is fair or unfair, and a great deal of thought to avoiding you, if possible, for ever more. He is also more than likely to go in for some behind the back criticism of his own and could, unless the situation is remedied with buckets of praise, quite likely brood on ways of getting even. During your career in Thailand, it is safer and more productive to forget anything you might have come to believe about the value of constructive criticism and to be aware that any criticism will have more negative than positive effects.

You might well have some adjusting and restraining to do if you are to function effectively in Thailand. This you could find yourself unable or unwilling to do. Some Western managers who are used to rule by fear, and enjoy things that way, love to argue that understanding Thai sensitivities to criticism is one thing while *pandering* to such sensitivities is quite another thing. Some go so far as to insist that a manager should not markedly change his behaviour patterns since he was selected for his post in Thailand because of his management track record, and he is responsible to his home office. Perhaps HQ sent him because the directors wanted something of a tough nut who would not be afraid to analyze the situation and to act on the analysis in a way that a Thai would find difficult to do. To cut out some dead wood and get the place in shape. If you are such a one, a muzzle could come in useful.

Criticism is not only disliked, it is regarded as destructive to the social system which keeps Thais together by keeping them apart. Be aware that the more you venture into criticism, the more the invisible weight of Thai social structure will move to crush your words. Nobody is more important than the system. Particularly the foreigner. Some special allowances might be made for you. But behave in a way that threatens the system and you will not accomplish great things.

The system assumes that decision comes from the superior. The inferior is supposed to obey. To criticise a superior is to question the role of the superior in the system. To criticise an inferior for anything other than failing to obey the superior's orders is equally destructive. To do so suggests either that the inferior is responsible for making decisions or that the orders given him by the superior are inadequate or that the superior has made a mistake in entrusting the job to somebody incompetent to do it. Thus, criticise an inferior and you not only make him lose face, you also make yourself lose face, since you are criticising yourself.

If a superior is criticised, in public or in private, he would most likely respond by removing the source of criticism. Thus, if you happen to be the inferior and wish not only to keep your job but also to suggest to a superior ways of saving money or lives, go very carefully. The difference between a suggestion and a criticism is subtle and subjective. No blunt letters pointing out that the benefits of your brilliant plan stand out a mile for anybody to see. Quiet, behind the scenes action which might not involve a word from you. You have a comprador and a staff. Use them. Then, when the big man comes out with *his* brilliant idea, you can say *that's super* and pledge your full support.

# CULTURE SHOCK

Culture shock can be bad for business. It affects
the way you think, feel, reason and interact. Ignore
it and it will not go away.

One of the peculiarities of our time is that a man or woman
can be uprooted from a familiar environment, flown halfway
around the world, dropped down in another time, climate
and culture, and be expected to get up the following day,
walk through the door into a strange office and function as
usual.

Like the fragile rice seedling, the human transplant
must either adapt and flourish in the new field, or wither
and perish. Unlike the pampered seedling, the expatriate
manager must survive without the loving care of an
experienced farmer and often without the comforting
company of other seedlings of the same stock. Not only
must he survive; he is expected to manage the unknown.

It is a great tribute to the human race that most people
in this position do carry on somehow. Indeed, many of
them revel in the novelty of their situation. But all feel at
least something of the disorientation known as culture
shock.

Culture shock can be bad for business. In addition to
everything else that comes with a new job in a new place,
you will have to live with it and try to minimize its effects

on your work. You have certainly made a good start by reading this book. Now buy the companion volume *Culture Shock Thailand*. It will help you and your family settle in, adjust and enjoy as quickly as possible. It will also boost the publisher's profits and increase my royalties. We have the essence of a fair deal. Everybody gains.

# DELEGATING

Delegation requires knowledge of your people, their abilities, status, popularity and, if appropriate, English language reporting skills. To acquire this knowledge will take longer than it did back home, but your time will be well spent. Bad delegation is difficult to correct later.

Very few management actions really matter very much and most hardly matter at all. This is not an excuse for saying *may pen rai*, or even never mind, closing this book and popping off for a beer. It is a recognition that priorities must exist in use of expensive expat manager's time and that a great many managers waste their time on routine matters. There is absolutely no point in trying to do what your Thai staff can do better than you, which is most things. And there is every reason not to waste your time, risk your status and offend your peoples' pride by showing them how to do what they already know how to do.

Delegating responsibility implies that you will judge performance by results. Before you hand out the work it is therefore well worth spending some time to make sure *you* understand what is to be done and the result expected. Then be prepared to spend as much or more time to make sure that the person to whom you are delegating responsibility fully understands what is required and is up to the task. To do this properly, you must know your people and their abilities. It will take you longer to acquire this knowledge than it did back home.

It is going to be quite difficult for you to get an idea as to an individual's suitability for a job, but this is essential before you make a decision. Time spent at the selection and explanation stages will save much time later. Any mistakes are the fault of the manager, not the delegate. Such mistakes can be expensive and correcting the situation can create bad feeling and take up much time.

When planning the delegation of responsibilities, exploratory discussion on a one-to-one basis is recommended. If you are satisfied that the person can do the job and would be reasonably happy to take it on, proceed to a full explanation. You might well find that a simple aide-memoire will help explanation and understanding, since some Thais read English much better than they speak it. Having selected a person for a responsibility, you will have to allow him the status to do the job without causing him embarrassment by obvious favouritism. Stepping out from his colleagues and above them can be difficult for a Thai.

Be prepared for the possibility that your chosen one might be rejected by those who should follow his orders for reasons that have nothing to do with ability to do the job and everything to do with the character and status, or lack of it, of the delegate. Your exploratory thoughts and discussions should take account of these factors. Popularity and respect are, in the Thai context, at least as important as ability to do the job.

Delegated work well done, even when it becomes routine, should be regularly lubricated by doses of praise. This provides assurance that work is being correctly done, an incentive to continue good work and perhaps improve certain areas that never get singled out for praise, makes you popular and keeps you in control. Remaining in control is essential. Praising makes it clear, in a nice and positive way, that you are aware of what your people are doing.

The English language poses a special problem when it comes to delegating responsibility. Your choice of the man for the job might get the results you want and have the full support of his work group. But the man might be unable to put together any report that makes much sense.

If regular written reports are required but do not come spontaneously, it is well worth spending some time to work out an appropriate standard format. Reporting on almost any activity can by this means be tailored to simple English and ensure that essential information is regularly supplied with the minimum of effort, time, ambiguity and loss of face.

In the Thai workplace, delegation can extend into non-professional areas. You need never fetch your own cup of coffee, go to the post office or take the car in for a clean and check. Somebody should be glad to do it for you. Such delegation of personal matters might well be forbidden or frowned upon back home but in Thailand it is an attribute of your comparatively high status and you should take full and reasonable advantage. The time you save will be significant and can be much better employed in more productive ways.

# DIFFERENCES

The world of business, like the social structure of
Thai society, is united and kept apart by differences.
You must learn what the differences are and how
to manage them.

An eye for an eye and a kilo of sugar for a kilo of sugar
might be scrupulously fair trading, but it does not hold
much interest for the trader. On the other hand, a kilo of
opium for a hundred kilos of rice or a glass eye for a set of
false teeth makes economic sense: both parties to the
trade stand to gain. Profitable trading must involve
qualitatively different goods or services.

Investment overseas is equally concerned with
differences rather than similarities. Any entrepreneur, at
home or abroad, is out to maximise profitable exploitation
of people and resources. He does this by buying cheap
and selling as expensive as the market will stand. He buys
labour and materials, brings them together and sells the
product of combination. There is nothing intrinsically nasty
about this process. In order to exploit labour in this day
and age, which has abolished slavery for sound economic
and humanitarian reasons, jobs must be created, wages
must be paid, training must be provided and, most
important for our considerations, people must be managed.
Everybody can gain from the trade in labour, resources

and knowledge, although it goes almost without saying that some will gain more than others. The investor who does not gain by putting his money in Thailand would put it elsewhere or keep it at home. Profitable expatriate investment must involve a labour force and/or resource materials significantly different to, and/or cheaper than, those existing in the home country.

Fortunately, Thailand and the Thais are different enough from other countries and peoples to make profitable trading and investment possible. Differences are an asset to be exploited, not a problem to be avoided. To profit from differences to the maximum, you must learn what they are and how to manage them.

# DISAPPEARING

You are likely to find yourself lost and perhaps angry when your Thai contact suddenly disappears. Thai norms on disappearance management are almost certainly different from what you are used to.

One of the things that most infuriates many foreigners working in Thailand is the way their Thai contacts, even business partners or regular interlocutors in a government ministry, can simply disappear upcountry or, if they are already upcountry, down to Bangkok, without a word. You have something urgent and important and you need contact, but all the secretary knows is that her boss has gone away. No contact telephone and probably only a vague idea of when he might be back. What a hell of a way to run a business!

You have noticed this tendency. Well, it is rather hard to miss. And you attribute it to a chap's personality or lack of proper management training. He is fine, pleasant, and you have no complaints except that having said goodbye in the afternoon you are never sure if he is going to be around the next morning. Now, when *you* go away, *you* let people know and you let everybody know who is in charge during your absence. Good sense, good management and good manners. Perhaps things would not be so bad if only he would leave somebody in charge. But nobody dares make any type of decision during his absence.

Eventually, you decide you just have to talk to him about this failing. Very politely, taking great care not to offend, you tell him what problems you had because he wasn't around the other day and you didn't know whom to talk to. He won't be offended. He has just received a compliment. Of course you had problems when he wasn't there to sort things out. He tells you when he is away you can always talk to Khun Taweechai. You leave with relief, probably congratulating yourself on getting the message home without damaging relations. After all, by now you are beginning to understand just how sensitive Thais can be when you suggest that maybe there is a little room for improvement in their conduct. So the next day you call him and his secretary tells you that he left for Singapore just after you saw him yesterday. Don't know when he'll be back. And of course you talk to Taweechai, who doesn't know either, and is as far as ever from delegated decision making.

Is this fellow serious? Can he be trusted? What kind of a monkey does he take you for?

The answers are Yes, Yes again, and a somewhat inferior monkey. Don't assume that because this key contact does not keep you posted on his whereabouts, he is not reliable and trustworthy. He is just playing things the Thai way. Maybe a little bit old fashioned if he is in business and wants to stay in business with foreigners. But if you are just a small part of his essentially Thai setup or if he is a government servant, then he is by no means out of date or out of step. And you will meet plenty more who behave in exactly the same way.

This seemingly cavalier conduct relates to the big man-little man basis of just about everything. The little person is responsible for keeping contact with the big and not vice versa.

The big man does not inform you when he is going off for a time. You are no longer annoyed, or you try your best to appear not to be, since you now understand the system. But how do you cope with it? Not so easy but not quite impossible. First, do not assume that the big man does not want to be found. Second, do not assume that everybody is as in the dark as you as to where he is and for how long he will be away. Members of his group could know, although he is not likely to have circulated details of his disappearing trick. Even more likely is that his direct superiors, assuming he has some and most people do, know precisely where he is. Since it is the task of the little people to maintain contact with the big, nobody can reproach you for trying to locate your superior. All the same, it is probably better and easier to have your comprador do the phoning around to her or his opposite numbers in the office of the big man's big man. When you find out where he is in Phuket, feel no compunction in calling to say, very nicely of course, what is on your mind. The last thing he would ever ask is *Where did you get my number?*

Thai norms on disappearance management are almost certainly different from what you are used to. But if you think carefully, aren't there some similarities? When you get back from your lunch across town three hours later than expected, to find your deputy and your accountant waiting urgently and politely to see you, think, did you let them know where you were? When it was obvious you would be late, did you make an attempt to call the office? Perhaps you did. But if you did not, nobody would think the worse of you.

The Thai system might not always be perfectly adapted to the modern world of business. Inconveniences must be lived with and nothing is to be gained by trying to hurry along changes in the system. Remember that many business contacts in Thailand are businessmen second and, publicly at least, something with a whole lot more status first, such as a professor at Chula or Thammasart universities, or an assistant to the Governor of Bangkok. Jobs which hardly pay enough to fill up the Benz but which ooze with and demand respect. A Thai doesn't change status as he moves from the university to the office. He might well be referred to in his office by the respect term for a learned man, even if he hasn't given a lecture in years. His status position is a compound. It gives him a place in a system which might sometimes appear anarchic to the expat manager but is really quite orderly. So much so in fact that it can even cope with what might seem to be the disappearance of key figures.

# ENGLISH

The problem is basic. You risk poor communications because of poor English and must find ways to be sure correct understanding takes place. Standardising language and report formats can assist understanding in most tasks. For important undertakings, a verification of understanding is necessary.

*I am being sell in Thursday with the car broken. Please request the permission send the car that walks in two at evening for to take me. Thank you very much.* A note sent in for your information or action from somebody you think is probably on your staff. Is the writer letting you know that he is being sold along with a broken car next Thursday? Was he out selling when the car broke down? Does he want you to request permission for whatever it is, or is he asking for permission? Does he want the walking car to pick him up at two in the evening, whenever that is, or does he want to use it at that time?

Faced with such puzzles on a daily basis, many expat managers, even those with English as their mother tongue, feel an overwhelming urge to scribble OK on the note and send it back where it came from, or anywhere at all away from their desk. Managers for whom English is a second language might waste much time trying to work out if there is something wrong with their understanding of the English idiom. Many such communications end up in the rubbish bin or being passed to a Thai staff member who also does not know what to do with them. The problem is basic. Poor communications because of poor English.

It must be faced and lived with that the level of English of most Thais leaves quite a lot to be guessed at. This is in spite of a comprehensive education system which includes English all the way through from pre-school to university. In terms of years, effort and often money, a tremendous investment is made in English. Why are the results so unsatisfactory? Perhaps the fact that teachers of English in the schools can rarely speak or understand the language and the rote learning methods give a clue to the answer.

Things are changing. Slowly. But a qualified secretary who is really fluent in English is still rare enough to command a salary above that of a general in the army or a university lecturer. And you will readily appreciate why. Our man who might have been sold along with a broken car could have explained everything in Thai to your secretary and you would have received, if it should come to you at all, an understandable interpretation in English.

Some good speakers and writers of English around you will prove invaluable and quite possibly indispensable. But you will still have to be prepared to spend a lot more time checking English (or Japanese, German, French, etc.) than you ever thought of doing back home. Try, however, to avoid revising everything that comes to you. Assume that nothing will be perfectly written. If it is understandable and not going up to important parts of the home office or outside to other agencies, let it go. Otherwise you will spend far too much time editing, and returning every draft that comes to you with corrections or a request to rewrite will not only waste the time of your staff but could cause loss of face and demoralisation.

Time wasted thus could be much better spent standardising the format of communications as far as possible. While standard formats can have certain disadvantages, the principal one being that your Thai drafter might leave out something new and important because it does not fit into the format, they are usually suitable for at least 90% of all routine work and greatly assist rapid communication.

You will find that initial communication problems, verbal or written, which seem to stump you over the simplest things, will get less frequent as you get used to Thai ways of speaking English, your staff get used to your way of speaking English and all of you fit into a routine where certain word patterns go along with specific actions. In no time at all you might surprise yourself with the realisation that you can manage a large organisation, seemingly complex tasks and lots of money with the basic vocabulary of a five-year-old plus a few technical terms, which as likely as not are the same in Thai and English.

A large portion of a manager's time should be spent on the non-routine, where standard language formulae cannot be relied upon. Here it is essential to make sure you have been understood. There is not much point in asking "do you understand?". Thais use the expression in Thai all the time and it marks the end of explanation rather than an invitation to ask questions. The person you wish to make understand will certainly have understood something and will assume it is what you wanted him to understand. So the answer yes means nothing at all.

Some expats find they need the reassurance of hearing orders or instructions repeated. Asking for a repetition of words does not guarantee understanding, but it is a lot safer than asking if somebody has understood you. The problem here is the embarrassment involved in grown people behaving like children. Never ask for such a verification in anything but a one-to-one situation. Instructions might be repeated perfectly, but it could look as if you do not have full confidence in the poor repeater. Even in private, you cannot use this technique very often without driving yourself crazy or, much worse, risking offence to somebody you need on your side. If you feel it is necessary to use such tactics, do so sparingly and make it clear that you distrust your own ability to explain something new and important and need to make quite sure that you are both thinking along exactly the same lines.

Not everything can be new and vitally important, so you need some alternative strategies to produce the reassurance result without constantly asking for repetition of what you just said, which makes you look a fool as much as anybody else. One simple method is to set down as simply and clearly as you can in writing precisely what you want done and send it to the staff member with a request that he study the instructions then come to discuss them with you. When he turns up clutching your memo, find a way of getting it out of his hands and have him verbally run through the process. "Not sure I understand this myself now, although it seemed clear enough when I wrote it. How would you go about it?" While simple repetition is not proof of understanding, it might be as close as you will get to finding out without participating in the action.

If something is really important, or even moderately so, it is a good idea to follow up as far as you can with an on-the-job inspection before things get to a point of no return. If everything is going right, praise will reassure, if some things are going right, praise those things and suggest, discreetly and privately, some changes where appropriate.

If everything is going wrong, and always seems to go wrong, there is probably something wrong with you, your command of English or your ability to explain. You might be in the wrong job in the wrong place. Even so, the Thais will help you through your time in the country. As long as you are a nice guy.

# ENTERING

If you find people hanging around your door, it might be that they are unaware of the formula to gain entry.

Thai staff demonstrate correct protocol and reinforce the social hierarchy by requesting permission to enter a superior's office. In Thai, this request follows a formula which is standard but which retains social meaning. It sounds strange if translated into English, mainly because Westerners usually content themselves with a knock on the door, even if it is open. Literally the formula translates *request permission* and is always followed by the respect particle *khrap/kha* and usually accompanied by a bow of the head.

The English equivalent to this would be something like *excuse me, am I disturbing you?* Few members of your staff are likely to be familiar with such speech patterns and are therefore prone to hang just inside the doorway, somewhat lost for words, waiting for you to look up from your desk and give a sign or word to indicate that they may enter. You can be sure that nobody likes to be left hanging and that most people will therefore exercise some self-restraint before disturbing you. Thus, Thai norms on entering a superior's space allow you to maintain a literal open-door policy without fear of constant interruptions.

Of course, a secretary making a dozen entrances a day to empty your out tray without disturbing you too much, and well used to foreign ways, will adapt to Western norms. The tea girl or boy, also a regular visitor, will probably not adapt and will request authorisation in Thai. Never mind if you don't understand the words, it is enough that they be said. A smile grants permission. Perhaps lifting your head from your papers will disturb the sacred managerial train of thought, but the brief ritual confirms that you are the boss. More importantly, you will not discover a cup of cold tea on your desk.

The Thai request to enter your physical world is one of the many symbols of respect which should punctuate your working day and give you that little lift that makes being a boss in Thailand so pleasant.

# FEEDBACK

To get feedback from your staff, you must make it
possible for them to talk to you in private.

Once somebody has screwed up his or her courage to
come and see you and has been granted permission to
enter your office, he might well be polite enough to be
reluctant to speak. For you, this is not likely to be
something you want to spend all day over. Go ahead and
ask the person to sit down and invite him to speak. Resist
the natural inclination for the big man, in this case you, to
do all the talking. It is all too easy to find that somebody
came to see you, you spoke, he left, and you have no idea
why he came. Do not waste an opportunity to get the
feedback you need from your staff, and to get it the Thai
way.

If you listen to your staff when they come to see you,
and perhaps do a little cultural interpretation of the
message, you will find you can obtain something of the
staff input into the running of your organisation that you
got back home through encouraging free and open
communication and discussion. The Thai system has the
advantage of discretion. You are quite free to say *I'll think
about it* and forget it. Nobody loses face and you remain
firmly in control.

If you allow Thai norms to predominate the workplace,

you will find it easier to keep your door open without this making impossible demands on your time. Respect should keep away those who have nothing to say. If, however, you encourage open equality and frank communication, you are likely to find that either nobody dares come to see you or that everybody wants to drop in and practise their English.

# FIRING

Good management can limit the need for firing people, but only up to a point. Firings usually fall into three categories: the redundant who should be financially compensated, the specialist who fails in his task and should be encouraged to resign, and the dishonest, who might require the expat manager to take on roles of judge and jury which are new to him.

The many books on how to manage people contain surprisingly little on how to fire people. Perhaps the assumption is that if people are well managed, there should be no need to fire any of them. If so, I would agree, but only up to a point.

To avoid the need for redundancies, the foreign company will need to research and plan its operations in Thailand, possibly to a greater extent than might be necessary back home. However, it will not be possible to foresee every political change. Political changes have economic consequences in any country and Thailand is certainly no exception; it might be enough for one minister to fall from grace for a market situation, and your staffing needs, to change overnight.

To avoid the need to fire a specialist who fails in his task, the foreign company would need to be particularly careful when hiring. The problem here is that you hire on the basis of professional or social qualifications because you need somebody who can do a job that you cannot do or interact in worlds to which you are a stranger. Whilst a manager's judgement of character comes into such decisions, it is far from infallible, particularly when faced with the Thai mask of charm. And many a daughter of an influential person has perfected, if little else in life, the ability to turn on the charm.

Firing people for dishonesty might be unnecessary if you had perfect security. However, you cannot watch every paper clip or the people who are supposed to watch the paper clips and more. In Thailand it has been known for organised security to become organised corruption. Dishonesty then becomes a normal part of daily activity and offers an expected supplementary income for otherwise quite honest people.

Cutting back on staff who have done no wrong and whom, if you are following suggestions contained in this book, you have encouraged to stay with you, is unpleasant. It happens. You will try to do it as fairly as possible. With a generosity which will not approach redundancy payments made back home but will be above what a Thai employee would expect. Money well spent because it maintains a measure of confidence among the staff who remain. If their turn comes, they will be fairly treated.

Dismissal for less than satisfactory performance poses much the same problems anywhere. Always allow the option of resignation, if possible whilst maintaining the financial compensation of termination. This option is often taken. It makes things easier for the resigning staff member when taking leave of other staff and easier for you, particularly if the departing is popular among the other staff. The difference between resignation and termination is perhaps a technical detail as far as you are concerned, but it is important to a Thai.

Firing somebody for dishonesty is often the most difficult and possibly dangerous of tasks. Many expat managers find themselves playing roles of judge and jury which are new to them. Some get a thrill from the novelty of the experience and the taste of naked power mixed with righteousness, others hate the whole thing. Back home such matters would probably have been taken care of by the personnel section and possibly by the police and a major concern would be to avoid accusations of unfair dismissal. Here in Thailand, unless your company has established alternative procedures, it is often better to handle the matter yourself.

If you are satisfied that your suspicions are well founded, inform the guilty that he is fired, make sure he hands in all keys, identification and so on and get him out immediately. You have made an enemy for life. On the other hand your action will meet with the approval of your staff and have worked towards minimum disruption of office harmony.

If you have more than one person to fire, take the advice of Machiavelli and do all of your dirty work quickly, that it can be more quickly forgotten.

In Thailand you can fire without fear of the victims making claims of unfair dismissal. Be well aware, however, that other ways of getting revenge exist.

# GIFTS

Gifts across cultural boundaries can lead to considerable bad feeling because of different points of view as to the correct form a gift should take and how it should be received, acknowledged and reciprocated.

You might be unwittingly excluded from much of the social interaction which gives life meaning and makes work endurable and often enjoyable for your Thai staff. You will certainly not be excluded from the inexorable round of giving and receiving presents. Generosity is a virtue with a very long tradition in Thailand. Whether you are giving to or receiving from a bigger or smaller person, the basic ground rules are the same. Learn them or you risk causing offence or feeling offended.

Apart from the regular and almost ritualistic exchanges of cakes and snacks that go on in any Thai workplace, gifts are almost always beautifully wrapped up. If you are handed a wrapped present on any occasion, do not rip apart the paper to see what is inside. That is being rude. People might forgive you as an ignorant foreigner who does not know better, but the sanctity of the act of giving has been destroyed. By all means thank the giver but put the gift aside and open it later when alone. You are not supposed to comment on the value of the gift. Not even to the point of saying *how lovely*, an expected statement and a sign of good manners in the West. After all, nobody would deliberately give you an awful present. Would they?

The fact that gifts are not examined in your sight does not mean that the contents go unnoticed. It also does not mean that you can wrap up just any old thing. Recycling of unwanted presents is all right, but it should be appropriately done, with reference to the comparative status of the recipient. This can be tricky. Under or over generosity can be embarrassing.

It can happen that a Thai member of your team will make a mistake and give you an expensive present that he or she is sure you will like. This is embarrassing for you. Quite possibly the giver sincerely appreciates you and wishes to express this in material terms. It would, however, be inappropriate for you to return a gift of equal value. That would suggest a special relationship between the two of you and could produce negative results for the team as a whole.

Having examined the gift in private, you might feel compelled to express your appreciation and thank the giver, otherwise you, not the giver, would feel uneasy. Go ahead, in private. But do not comment on the value. Do not say *You should not have done it*, which would likely be interpreted literally and discourage the giver. *Never* return or refuse a gift, even if you are sure the giver could not afford it. And do not automatically assume that the giver expects something back in return. At least not immediately. In fact, the act of expressing your appreciation for the gift in itself provides some indication that it will not be reciprocated. On the other hand, expressed thanks for a gift can also suggest to a Thai mind that you want more of the same. So be careful.

Reciprocity in gift exchange between Thais can take a lifetime. Your time span of reciprocity is likely to be much abridged and more clearly relate to an exchange of business favours. However, you will still exchange gifts. More than just an annual Christmas card and calendar is expected if you are doing business with somebody. Alcohol is always appropriate, even if the recipient does not drink. *Not* a bottle of Mekhong whisky but something with status ranging between Black Label and a very good brandy. An assumption is made here that the recipient is male. For

"MERRY CHRISTMAS"

the rare occasion when you would be gifting a lady, perfume, a stationery set, or similar luxury items, are all fine as long as they have a well-known Western brand name and are the genuine article, not labelled up in a sweat shop in Thon Buri.

A cause of major misunderstanding between Thais and foreigners living in Thailand occurs when a gift is sent instead of being handed over. Acknowledgments are not made. This can upset the foreigner, who might feel that the seemingly ungrateful Thai recipient is either taking generosity for granted or perhaps was unhappy with the present.

On a purely pragmatic level, you might be left wondering if your gift ever arrived or if the messenger substituted a bottle of local whisky for your $80 bottle of finest brandy. To the non-Thai, it seems rude not to acknowledge with thanks a gift made. To the Thai, the same rationale applies for unsolicited gifts received through the post or by messenger as for those handed over personally and put to one side unopened. Appreciation might be felt but is not expressed.

Be aware that ruptures of friendships, budding business relationships and love affairs have occurred because a foreigner has felt rebuffed after receiving no acknowledgment for his generosity. There is little room for compromise between opposing views on what constitutes correct behaviour by the recipient of a gift. If you want at least to be sure that your present arrived in the hands of the person to whom it was intended, give it yourself.

# GOSSIP

Most office gossip is not a lot of use to you. In-group gossip between businessmen and politicians could be very useful.

Thais are not all angels. The world of surface harmony that you see around your place of work is no doubt riddled with office gossip of all kinds. Never mind. As long as you have surface harmony and working relations appear to be good, that should be all that matters to you.

Equals communicate freely within the office and outside it. Occasionally so do non-equals. If you find yourself apprised of the progress of the affair between Pong and Pui every time your secretary brings your morning tea, this is not a sign of equality but of a secretary who cannot keep her mouth shut. Do not listen to such gossip with any hope of getting useful feedback on the way your staff is thinking; the gossiper will certainly edit out any references to management. Anyway, she would make the worst kind of spy since everybody will be aware of her propensity to inform and she is just as likely to gossip about you. You would be well advised to shut her up. Politely if possible. As soon as she starts into a subject and you see another half-hour of your time going down the drain, ask her to get you so-and-so on the line. Next time try the same trick or send her to the other end of the building to get a file that doesn't exist. If she does not catch on, you will have to be less than polite. If it comes to it tell her, I am sorry but I just do not have time for tea *and* gossip, and thanks for the tea, which is just the way I like it.

Gossip is greatest within a peer group and criticism is usually reserved for individuals outside of one's own group. Businessmen, politicians, government servants and influential persons who have developed a group-based mutual trust relationship are certainly no exception. Their in-group gossip, unlike most of that which goes on within your office, could be important to your company. You will almost certainly not be a party to such gossip. Your comprador might pick up enough leads to give you an idea what is going on behind the scenes and behind your back. Be aware that some quite incredible deals, not always within the letter of the law, begin as chit-chat and go through solely on the basis of group trust, without a single word written down.

# HIRING

Time spent selecting the right people is time saved. Verify all shortlisted candidates by test and interview and keep in mind that some jobs have more importance than they might merit back home. Be aware of the utility of peer group evaluation.

As any book on management will tell you, the manager's most precious resources are time and people. For once, I agree. It follows that you will be prepared to invest time in selecting the kind of people who will do a reasonable job and save you time later. Hiring is always something of a gamble but you can stack the cards in your favour by taking account of special emphases in the Thailand situation.

In addition to selecting an applicant who can do the work, perhaps with some on-the-job training, you will be looking for somebody with a personality likely to click in the team and/or with outsiders including foreigners, and likely to remain with you for some time.

Advertising might seem to be the best way to reach the most able. It is not without disadvantages. Do not automatically advertise all openings in the English language media: first consider whether English is important for the job. A cook in the canteen, a nightwatchman, a cleaner can probably work perfectly well without speaking

English. You want reliable people, not somebody who reads the English language papers. If the coffee girl needs to recognise the words tea, coffee, sugar, milk and the lift boy needs to be able to say "what floor, sir/madam", and understand the number given, it is a waste of time, money and talent to advertise for an English speaker when ten minutes of language instruction would suffice. Do not automatically add *English speaking* to every vacancy notice. Consider advertising in Thai.

As a general policy, which takes into full account the realities of English comprehension among the population, saves you time and money, reduces risks of breaches of confidentiality and helps the less educated find employment, the level of English required for a particular job should not be significantly above the minimum necessary to do that job well.

Most of the many replies to your advertisement in the English language press will be inappropriate. Specify that a knowledge of Japanese is essential and you will wade through piles of applications that give no indication of speaking a word of the language.

On the other hand, most applications will provide you with plenty of irrelevant information. This is not the applicant's fault. Thai companies often routinely require such information as hobbies, religion and race (meaning ethnic origin). You will notice that many of the applicants spend as much time to let you know that they can sing-a-song, play guitar and take part in various sports, as in addressing the list of qualifications you set out in your advertisement. The majority of applications for almost any job important enough to advertise can be discarded with little thought apart from the occasional conscience pang as you glance at the young hopeful's photograph, which, requested or not, inevitably graces the CV and in many cases is the best thing about it.

The well presented and appropriate CV will certainly stand out. It might come complete with copies of very fancy certificates from schools which do not seem to have a phone number and certified lists of grades achieved in all kinds of subjects. There might even be a letter of recommendation from an expat manager who, it turns out when you phone, unfortunately returned to Norway three months ago. By all means shortlist the candidate, but reserve judgement until you have interviewed personally and verified that the person really can type at six hundred words per minute, knock off your monthly accounts before

I'M STUDYING FOR MY THIRD PhD, I GO HOT AIR BALLOONING, MY... MY DOG IS BLACK, I WENT TO HARVARD, I WROTE D-BASE AND LOTUS 123, I BREED RACING ELEPHANTS, AM VERY HONEST AND WOULD MAKE A GREAT COMPANY DRIVER

morning coffee, and ride a one-wheeled bicycle through an impressive array of social contacts collecting goodwill all the way. Be aware that some candidates have the initiative to exaggerate their skills somewhat and get more than a little help with their applications.

Advertise without a box number, specifying that applications must be in writing, and you will find your entrance hall blocked with people trying to see you to plead their case. Some of them will get through. Do you applaud their initiative or scrub them from the list?

Why, you will ask yourself, in an expanding economy, are so many people so keen to take whatever job you advertise? And where does this leave the central argument of this book, that cultural factors are important to productive management, when it seems as if everybody is very keen indeed to work in a foreign company and under a foreign boss? In two words, the answer is *status*, which is a cultural factor even if the high status company is non-Thai, and *money*, since advertising in the English language media is usually, but not always, reserved for the better paid or higher status jobs.

There is a third reason, particularly relevant to young applicants, which might be called blanket-coverage; a belief that by sending off applications to as many places as possible, something must eventually get through, particularly if a vow is made to pay for a troupe of dancers to entertain the elephant god if the gamble pays off. While you are discarding and shortlisting, the elephant god, who might have been approached by a number of candidates, will be doing his own selection according to the value of the vows made. This is why you get the feeling that hiring people involves playing god.

Having retained the minority of appropriate applications, it is time to have people in for interview and selection. How much time you give will depend on the importance of the job. Some jobs might have an importance in Thailand that they would not have back home. A telephone operator who not only has the patience to grapple with Bangkok's overloaded telephone system but also speaks good English and has a pleasant personality can save you a lot of money by making quick and correct connections on expensive overseas telephone calls and improve your image with other foreign companies in Thailand. Certainly worth more of your time and thought than you might consider appropriate back home.

If it is important for the successful applicant to work as part of a team, use the team as part of the selection mechanism. Surprisingly, this is rarely done. More usual is for the selected to be introduced to the team as their new member after being given the job. Of course the decision on employment is yours and you do not democratically call in the votes before coming to it. But it makes sense to show the applicant what he or she will be doing and with whom it will be necessary to work. It does happen that ten minutes together is enough to suggest reservations or indicate suitability. And perhaps the Thai team, who will have to work with the successful candidate and be in part evaluated on the basis of that person's contribution, will be somewhat less swayed than the expat manager by the candidate's personal charm.

# INCENTIVES

Incentives should be aimed at encouraging long term employment and maintaining a consistent and happy team. The most effective incentives on an individual basis are often those which cost nothing.

In Thailand, low pay, expanding opportunities and continuing links with the seasonal labour and social commitments of home villages incline many workers to job hop. If you can encourage long term employment, you will gain a more experienced, consistent and in many ways more loyal workforce. Whether on the workshop floor or in the office, constant staff turnover is disruptive and time and money is lost in recruiting and retraining. Consistency of employment and productivity tend to go hand in hand. Incentives should therefore be aimed at creating and maintaining a consistent and happy team rather than emphasising individual competition and individual rewards.

Incentives to remain in the job and to work well in a team should be tangible. Forget any sophisticated ideas about employee share holding or partnership bonuses. The concept of shares is understood within only a very small circle and even the highly educated Thai elite generally feels happier putting its money into land or visible capital than into shares. Cash payment bonuses, by contrast, act as a significant incentive to remain in the job.

Annual bonuses work best and timing for the new year fits in with existing patterns of gift giving. By all means maintain a differential between your staff. Several formulae exist, the simplest being to give everybody an extra month's salary if they have been with you throughout the year (*pro rata* for comparative newcomers, to give them a taste of the fruits to be had if they stay put): thus, while everybody gets the same in terms of one month's extra pay, the more senior receive proportionately more than their juniors. If you are afraid of a post payment mass exodus, make it clear that the bonus will be retained from salary owed if an individual leaves within three months of its payment.

Monthly productivity bonuses are a waste of money and could be counter productive. They simply become part of expected salaries and variation downwards appears as reduction in the pay packet, which will be resented and result in decreased rather than increased efforts to raise productivity. Monthly bonuses do nothing to encourage longer term employment, are complicated to administer and understand and do not conform, as do annual bonuses, to Thai norms of patronage downwards in exchange for consistent and loyal service upwards.

An ideal complement to annual presents is the provision of daily incentives. A variety exist, but the most important relate to food. If your company is big enough, an array of traditional fast food sellers will crop up in a location near your enterprise. The lowest paid of your workers will fill up on noodles or rice with a little something on top and lashings of fish sauce. They do so because it is cheap. It is also inadequate in terms of dietary needs and not the best basis for an afternoon of productive labour. Providing a nice, clean canteen will not act as any incentive to the more modest of your staff unless nourishing meals are provided at cost or subsidised. It is unfortunately common in Bangkok to find catering contracts in company canteens sold to the highest bidder. Thus many companies seem to their workers to be making money from the fact that everybody must eat.

Food is not simply a form of energy to get the work done. In Thailand it has symbolic and emotive values. Traditionally, those who work together also eat together, at the expense of the host farmer or employer. Your company cannot reproduce the ambience of traditional life, but food perks can act as a daily indication of the company's interest in the worker's welfare and provide an incentive to stay on rather than move to another job which does not include such benefits.

A productive workforce is not only well-fed, it is also healthy. A medical benefits scheme, even with what might seem to you to be a very low annual ceiling and none too generous reimbursement maximums of 70%, will be much appreciated by your lower-paid workers, who usually have no health insurance at all.

Other incentives to remain in your employment include the provision of free uniforms and, for those getting their hands dirty, overalls. Free or no-profit transportation is also greatly appreciated and although this might not be practical to arrange within central Bangkok, it could be an essential if you are located far outside.

Some of the best incentives cost very little or nothing

at all. It is not too difficult to arrange that monthly salaries are paid in the third week of the month rather than at the end. It costs you no extra and allows your people to have their monthly fling a little ahead of the rest of the world, when the restaurants and shops are empty instead of full and when bargaining is most effective. Similarly, arranging production schedules to allow those of your people who originate from the North or Northeast to take leave and return home over the three-day Songkran period (Thai New Year, 13–15 April), need not cost anything and could save money by planning for absences which will anyway occur.

Financial incentives of any kind are likely to be too low to produce much effect on many of your higher status personnel. The comparatively high salary of the general's daughter in the public relations department might go some way towards defraying the cost of the fancy Western fashions in which she turns up to work but would not cover the cost of her perfume, were she ever to buy it herself. She will shrug shoulders at canteen facilities, medical schemes and even the annual bonus. But she will be ensnared, if you want her to be ensnared, by a fancy name card, which costs you practically nothing. On the card it costs the same to write Assistant to the Public Information Officer as it does to put Head of Public Information Research, yet the second is much more likely to generate pride in the job. It is also far more likely to open doors to contacts and could therefore be justified in terms of functional productivity as well as an individual status-boosting reward. Similarly, if your Public Information

Officer is doing a good job, why not make him into a Director of Public Information?

When looking for low-cost incentives, remember the basic guidelines. Work should be pleasant and provide ample opportunities for social encounter through arranging activities to fit work group patterns whenever possible. The pleasant should blossom into open fun regularly enough for your people to feel more than a simple economic connection with their work. Parties can be effectively linked to celebrations related to the festive/religious calendar, (merit-making *khatin* bus trips, the blessings of monks for the prosperity of the company and staff), or to group congratulation of a staff member selected for promotion or a spell of training in Head Office, or simply getting married or having a baby. Praise, of course, should flow and criticism be tightly controlled. A letter of commendation signed by a director for something particularly well done is worth its weight, or more, in gold when it comes to inciting the recipient to work even harder for the company that notices its people and cares about them.

# INTRODUCTIONS

Introductions tend to be more functionally specific
in Thailand than in the West. The correct order of
presentation is inferior first.

Back home, a guest or visitor to a party or the office is
introduced to everybody within range and forgets all of
them immediately. In Thailand, don't worry at all if you
are not introduced to everybody, or even to anybody.
Nobody is snubbing you. It is simply that blanket
introductions without any clear purpose are not Thai
convention. If you think you might like to know someone,
on the other hand, there is no need to wait to be introduced.
Thai protocol allows you to ask somebody for his or her
name and to give yours.

A formal introduction by a third party is normally used
only if there is a reason for the people involved to know
each other. As a busy manager in a strange social
environment, you should readily appreciate that this saves
you wasting time on people of no relevance. Such
introductions conform to the status structure and should
make relative status positions immediately evident because
the inferior is addressed first. "Khun Daniel this is Khun
Somchai, your contact person in the Ministry of Interior".
Khun Daniel *wai* first.

Note that the ordering of formal introductions is the

reverse of polite convention in Western countries, where the most important person would normally be addressed first. Although speaking English, get into the habit of using, and responding appropriately to, the Thai speech habit. Nobody is likely to be offended if you get things muddled up. But getting things right can only help you.

# JAPANESE

The Japanese are willing to fit within the existing framework of business cum politics, to treat their people well in order to retain their services and encourage dependency linked with dependability. They are usually a success.

Pop into Toyota's service stations in Bangkok or Chiang Mai around eight in the morning and you will see everybody who works in the plant standing in neatly uniformed lines to attention for the Thai national anthem. Behind them writ large upon the walls in Thai are the rules that all should follow. When the music stops, the human lines remain in place and, under the direction of a Thai manager, go through a set routine of physical exercise.

This is the way to begin the day. It does not seem at all Thai, and, apart from the national anthem bit, it is not. Yet, clearly, most Thais involved like it. Evidence perhaps that some foreign concepts and ways of doing things can be usefully introduced into the Thai work world.

Pop into Sogo Department Store in Bangkok and you will find the Japanese manager speaking to his Thai staff in Thai. The Head Office in Tokyo had thought it worthwhile for a Japanese coming to work in Thailand to know the basics about Thai language and Thai culture.

There are significant similarities between Thais and

Japanese. For a start, they both have a lot of trouble mastering the English language and the spoken forms of each other's languages. When it comes to non-verbal communications, many of the outward signals of respect are similar enough to allow both sides to feel at ease in translating symbols. The Japanese use of the bow is near enough to the Thai use of the *wai* to allow substitution: the Westerner's use of the egalitarian handshake on the other hand, is very different to Thai use of the *wai* and cannot be readily substituted without communicating a different message to that intended. Japanese and Thai sensitivities are also similar enough that offence can be recognised and avoided. Even the male Japanese penchant for letting off steam through the use of alcohol and women, which has given the Japanese a negative image in many countries, including Thailand, is near enough to the behaviour patterns of many Thai men.

There are also very significant differences between Thais and Japanese. It is very difficult to imagine Thai workers requiring persuasion to take holidays due to them; a mania for long, continuous, hard work is none too evident among the various traits of Thai personality. To this basic difference in work ethics we must add a long influence from the West, initially from England on the political system and later in the form of something like a special relationship with the United States. It is also most relevant that Thai youth, encouraged by the media and the long years spent trying to pick up some English, Thailand's dominant foreign language, is much more orientated towards the West than towards Japan or other Asian cultures. Add it all up and it is by no means easy to explain the remarkable success of Japanese companies in Thailand.

The Japanese success seems to relate to two things, a willingness to fit in with the existing framework of business cum politics and a willingness to treat people well and value long term service. Perhaps the oft quoted perceptions of Gunnar Myrdal from his 1968 classic *Asian Drama* are still relevant; in that work, Myrdal makes a convincing argument that the Japanese in Asia are the most willing of foreign companies to pay bribes to secure trading and manufacturing advantages over their competitors and to ensure the smooth day-to-day running of their organisations. (Myrdal suggests that the West Germans, French and Americans also pay up, but somewhat less willingly and less generously.)

At least as important as providing incentives to influential Thais to assist in setting up in an alien economy, is the Japanese recognition that, whilst their companies cannot (yet) offer the workforce life-long employment following anything like the model in Japan, they can and do spend a lot of money on the welfare of their employees, provide them with social activities and perks and send a selection to Japan for training. All of this encourages workers and staff to identify with their company.

The Japanese do not have a secret formula to apply universally and ensure good results. Managers of companies established in Thailand are encouraged to learn about Thai ways of doing things and to adapt the Japanese model accordingly. They keep their people happy and work through the system. You can do much the same.

# KICKBACKS

The expectation of payment in return for special favour is widespread and goes way beyond the concept of tipping. Intermediaries are usual and kickbacks are normally shared out to all involved in granting a favour, including those you may never see.

Few Thais openly support bribery and corruption but few would refuse a present offered for a service rendered.

Foreign businessmen are equally reluctant to admit participation in giving and receiving kickbacks. Most are aware, however, that if they want to make sure their tender for a contract gets selected, or even gets fairly considered, they must have somebody, somewhere, looking after their interests with an incentive greater than that inspired by the basic wage, which is always too low. On a much reduced scale, small amounts of money are regularly needed to oil the wheels of industry. Refuse to provide your truck drivers with quantities of small bank notes and your trucks will be stopped and searched at every police checkpoint. A few more notes will probably be needed to get your goods cleared in time to be loaded onto the ship. And a few more to make sure it is the correct ship.

The larger scale kickbacks either occur regularly within an in-group or involve go-betweens. The efficient comprador will let you know in confidence when somebody requires *money to open the mouth* (to speak in favour of and actively pursue your interests). By so doing, your comprador serves much the same function as a marriage go-between did in the early stages of marriage negotiations in the past and prevents embarrassment to either party.

In the absence of, or in addition to, a professional comprador's network of contacts, specific-purpose intermediaries arise from time to time. A clerk in a government office might turn up on behalf of his superior and inform you or, more likely, your assistant, that a specific sum of money is required before a service can be performed. There is not much chance of finding out if the clerk and your assistant are telling the truth and this is why the kickback, or at least the major portion of it, is only paid on successful completion of the service. Such an intermediary, like many a businessman, is a speculator. If he fails to come up with the results, he gets nothing.

In general there is honour among the corrupt. The bribe will be shared out, in amounts reflecting status, to all involved in granting a favour. The top man will perhaps appear on the scene briefly or not at all, but will receive a large slice of the pie. Occasionally things do not work this way. A comparatively junior member of an organisation's staff actively involved in drawing up bids for a contract might be able to provide valuable information on the competition and present your bid favourably. Take care before entering any understanding. If the young man or woman is trying to step outside of the honour system and is found out, at the time or later on, it would certainly do him or her no good and could reflect on your enterprise. Better to stay within the system.

There is also more to corruption than money alone. Even if you are willing to top any kickback that the opposition can offer, there is very little chance of you being accepted in place of a regular, known and trusted member of the in-group. Unless you have already agreed to sub-contract that particular member at very generous terms. This is one way into the contract game and prominent contractors are often happy enough to keep a low profile by "sub-contracting". Another way in is for you to approach whoever will win the contract, and guessing ahead is often not so difficult, with an offer to sub-contract at terms which are favourable to him.

Expat companies and organisations not only pay out kickbacks in order to obtain benefits, they can also be victims of the system. If you want to make sure that your company's business goes to the cheapest or the most efficient quotation, you will have to be prepared to do more than simply cast an eye over the ritual opening of envelopes. Not so easy to do when many of the submissions seeking your favour are written only in Thai.

Kickbacks, given or received, are invisible. They exist but do not appear in anybody's books except in heavy disguise and you do not mention them to the main recipients or donors. It is therefore difficult and perhaps pointless to guess whether the incidence of bribery is higher in Thailand than elsewhere.

The act of accepting kickbacks is referred to in Thai as *eating*. And in Thailand as elsewhere, everybody has to eat.

# LEARNING THAI

A little Thai learnt well can create a good impression and leave people guessing as to how much you understand. A lot of Thai spoken badly or inappropriately can have the opposite effect, although no Thai will tell you so.

To learn Thai, you need time, lots of it. You will also need an interest in and respect for Thais and their language. Most expats are in the country for three years, have little in the way of spare time and prefer to spend what they have with family and common language friends. They are not encouraged to learn by their employers and after one or two attempts with books which barely relate to the sounds of Thai or with Thai language teachers who barely relate to foreigners, find that even to think about learning Thai is too exhausting.

For those who do continue with the basics, there is a problem of persuading people to talk to you in Thai. Anyone who does not look Asian is addressed, if at all, in English, usually of a tortured kind. People do not expect you to speak Thai and will probably not recognise that your early attempts at the language are supposed to be Thai. If they do, they will compliment you on your astounding cleverness in speaking their language, but will most likely have to guess at what you are trying to say, and very often guess wrongly. Order a stuffed omelette and the waitress brings you a beer.

The more sophisticated and educated will either speak to you in English which, if not perfect, is a lot better than your Thai, or feel the impossibility of saying anything interesting in Thai because your level of comprehension and response is not up to it. This psychological barrier is very difficult to cross. You have only crossed it when you trust yourself to negotiate without an interpreter in Thai: possible for the Chinese speaking and looking foreigner to envisage within six-twelve months but for most Westerners and Japanese a very long and tough job indeed.

You should not be put off learning at least enough Thai to get through the simplest acts of life without needing to be continuously accompanied by an interpreter. But however fluent you are in English, French, German, Swedish and so on, do not assume that you will learn Thai quickly. That would only cause you discouragement when you fail. Be prepared to spend a lot of time on the basics.

To brief you, hopefully without frightening you off, here are some very basic facts about the Thai language. Grammar is simple, everything else is difficult. Thai is usually classed within the Chinese family. It is, however, not a very close relative. Even the Chinese speaker could have trouble with final consonants and vowel lengths which do not exist in Chinese. There are five tones in the official, Central, form of Thai taught in school and generally used in Bangkok: mid, low, falling, high, rising. Most of the consonants have aspirated and non-aspirated forms, which accounts for the fact that there are usually said to be forty four (sometimes forty six) consonants in the Thai alphabet. Vowels are no less of a problem, with twenty nine symbols or symbol-clusters in the alphabet, long and short forms of all vowels, and vowels which are spoken but not written. The alphabet is based on Sanskrit and is not much more phonetic than is the roman alphabet when used for English. There is no standard romanised script for Thai.

Are you still with me? Then you had better know that mastering all the technicalities and vocabulary problems of Thai is not enough unless you take account of very different speech habits existing between Thai and English. These can be as simple as different ways of expressing such mundane things as hello, goodbye, please and thank you and as complex as the Thai social system of status stratification. English gets by with one pronoun for *you*

and one for *I*, most European languages get by with two for each, Thai has at least a dozen ways of saying you and almost as many ways of saying I. If you are right at the top and talking to or about royalty, the Buddha, Buddha images or monks, then you should really be using a very different and altogether higher form of Thai.

If you have only a limited time, you might decide that it is better to learn, from a good teacher, a few phrases well rather than a lot of words badly. A little Thai spoken correctly, or almost so, and appropriately, will create a good impression and leave people guessing as to how much Thai you understand. Let one of your perfect phrases be along the lines that you are trying to learn the beautiful Thai language but realize that the person you are speaking to speaks excellent English and therefore you will not offend his ears by your bad pronunciation. Such basic diplomatic Thai gives you every excuse for switching into English.

Nothing is worse than the foreigner who insists on speaking bad pidgin Thai to somebody who speaks good English. Such not only offends the ears but also risks causing deeper offence, since the content, if it is understood, could be inappropriate. Of course, no Thai will tell you to shut up. Not even when you make a fool of yourself and embarrass everybody by speaking to the lift boy as if he were a very important person or speaking to an important person as if he were the lift boy. If you are going to say inappropriate things, say them in English.

# LETTERS

Formal letters retain something of the mystique and authority of the past, when the written word was reserved for the educated and powerful. Form is important. It is also in your interest to send letters in Thai and keep both Thai and non-Thai versions for reference.

Communication, verbal or written, is traditionally initiated upwards in terms of a request or polite petition for assistance and downwards in the form of orders, authorisation or judgement.

As literacy has increased in the twentieth century, upward written requests have been standardised and the large Thai bureaucracy now has a form for almost anything you can think of, and some things you would never guess at. Downward written authorisations have also become routine, although they have lost little of their association with power and legitimacy. Every Thai keeps safely his identity card and house registration, without which his recognition as a citizen of Thailand is in question and he can do very little without contravening the law.

Communication by letter still occasionally takes the form of a written petition upwards signed by a number of representatives of the staff or workers, or perhaps farmers or squatters displaced by the extension of your enterprise. Such petitions are polite requests with no suggestion of threat. Do not ignore them. Often a question of money is involved and polite bargaining is expected. Sometimes it is a question of public relations. Much better to meet the farmers, show them around your factory and let them see for themselves why you are 100% sure that waste disposal precautions are so advanced that their fears of pollution of the rice fields are groundless. To confirm that your confidence is well placed, you will offer to pay for an independent agricultural expert to examine their fields as often as they wish. Don't forget to have some snacks and drink on hand for the apres-tour and to contribute generously to the village temple renovation fund or school sports facilities.

Letters written for official or business purposes are always formal in style. Don't try for jokes. And even if the person you are writing to speaks super English, it is a good idea to send the original in Thai, with the English version headed *translation* and attached. Your comprador will translate the original from your translation.

There is more to this than simply being polite. It is quite possible that the excellent English speaker to whom you are writing does not open and read all letters himself, or draft replies to them himself. He might also want to circulate your letter within his organisation before answering. Or he might simply not feel up to replying in English, even if his comprehension and spoken language is good. Thais writing in English more often than not leave unintentional ambiguities and unclear meanings. It is embarrassing to both sides to have to seek clarifications. If your letter is in Thai, it is possible that you will get a reply in Thai quickly and to the point. Translation then becomes the responsibility of your office not his: and it is much easier to ask your own staff for clarification, if necessary. A letter sent only in English could wait a long time for an answer.

You must also plan for the possibility that your English speaking contact might be replaced by one who inherits a file on your company full of communications in English that he does not really understand and which perhaps make him feel inadequate. Rather than risk loss of face, such a contact is not likely to go to a lot of effort to try to understand. And if a letter is not read, no communication has taken place, although you might think it has.

# MEETINGS

Meetings usually follow a ritual format that allows for zero spontaneity. Directives are given and an amount of information might be exchanged. The higher ups will make noises and possibly statements in the game of follow the leader; the lower downs will quietly take note. Expect no brainstorming.

The typical Thai meeting follows a ritual routine that many foreigners find boring in the extreme. The more a meeting is important, the more it serves ritual purposes, the less gets said and the fewer questions there will be. At very, very important meetings, nothing gets said at all. Or so it seems.

A very important meeting is opened by a very big man, who makes a few non-remarkable remarks or reads at greater length from a prepared speech, and who then sits and reads out names and functional titles of participants each of whom stands and bows in acknowledgement. The very big man might allow participants to introduce themselves, which they will do in low respectful voices that cannot be heard.

Having sanctified the meeting, the very big man might hand over the chair and leave or he might not. Participants then give out their information which has been prepared in advance. Any non-prepared statements or questions will come from the most important people present, who will also carry any conclusions. Leaving meetings for any reason, even to go to the toilet, requires standing to something like attention and bowing to the chair to indicate a request for permission to leave. The purpose of such meetings is to demonstrate the importance of the main message and conformity of opinion and action in pursuit of the goal.

You will probably not want to follow the ritual format, at least for internal meetings, but you should be prepared for the fact that meetings are not likely to be quite like the ones back home.

The Thai reluctance to criticise or to risk being criticised extends to asking questions. Since any question asked in a staff meeting, workshop or training session could suggest either that the information provided by the boss or his delegates was less than perfect or that the questioner was incapable of understanding, very few questions ever get asked. This becomes increasingly the case the more you mix up status levels within a single meeting. Such acquiescence can be quite useful when you want to convey clearly to everybody what line should be followed. The higher ups will make noises and possibly statements in the game of follow the leader; the lower downs will quietly take note. Expect no brainstorming.

Use meetings for exchanges of information and informing of directives. There are other ways of getting peoples' views and ideas. Do not expect a junior staff member to voice any good, or bad, ideas or hint of a complaint at a public meeting. Use the time you save by avoiding unnecessary meetings to leave your door open for staff to consult you in private. If appropriate, you might incorporate points of privately provided information meriting common concern in the next staff meeting, without making any reference to the source unless it is to praise without risking embarrassment.

Working within the system in this way takes no more time than trying to be smarter than everybody else in overlong and often unnecessary meetings of the type you had back home.

You might genuinely miss, or you might pretend to miss, the cut and thrust of dialectical debate, but you will come to appreciate that the Thai system, at least as far as meetings are concerned, is a lot easier on the nerves. It is also, when you don't know off the top of your head the answer to a question, a lot safer.

# MISTAKES

Mistakes involve loss of face. One way to avoid making many is to do very little. When your people make them, enlist their help to rectify the situation.

Few people in this world really aim for the moon and most tend to play their jobs and careers safe and slow rather than risk a total eclipse. Probably, compared to Westerners, but not compared to Japanese, Thais have a greater tendency to play it safe. In *general*, Thais will not launch themselves into initiatives in the hope of scoring with the boss unless they know they are on solid ground. To fail would mean a mistake had been made and a recognised mistake would mean loss of face. Whether in the realm of entrepreneurial venture or workplace productivity, commendable initiatives and disastrous mistakes are not likely to strike you between the eyes every day.

Even playing for safe, everybody makes a mistake now and again. You will certainly make plenty and not even realise it. Your staff will, hopefully, have too much respect for you, or for your position, to point out the error of your ways. So you could repeat your mistakes until they become evident even to you. If your Thai staff like you, they will cover up for you before too much of a mess is made. If, however, you charge into your new job with lots of innovations, your staff might mistake your mistakes for your new ways of doing things.

If this happens *and* nobody particularly likes you, then you have got yourself into a situation from which it is very difficult to retreat without loss of face. You will possibly end up blaming your staff for mistakes which are yours or started with you and were faithfully followed by your people. If you can't go back to France immediately, the only way out is to call a moratorium on any new activities, take your staff, at your expense, on a very nice day cruise to Ayudhya, give them plenty to eat and drink and tell them clearly that you think every single one of them is an absolute gem.

As manager, you would probably like to think that you are being paid to do a little more than take your staff on trips up the river and simply sign your name at the bottom of letters, cheques, account sheets and reports prepared by others. Your bosses, whether in Thailand or the home country, would probably like to think so too. However, there is often a very large gap between what managers and their overlords *think* they do and what they *do* do. At the risk of heresy, I would say that the "blind signer" type player in the management game is engaged in a course of action less dangerous than it sounds. Plenty of expats have signed their way happily through a very pleasant stay in Thailand.

If you have never really understood all the bits of paper that come to you and will only go away when you sign them, there is probably not much point in trying to get to know them in Thailand. Sign away. Let things continue as they were before you and will be after you. At least your people will like you. And if you do nothing, you are less likely to make mistakes. Doing very little is the best way for certain types of manager to maintain and increase productivity; and as long as somebody monitors that basic objectives are met, and as long as visitors from home are shown that everything is running smoothly and given a good time, Headquarters are most unlikely to start looking for your mistakes. And if they do, they won't find any.

Management by minimum activity is likely to be far less disruptive than management by mistakes. If you consistently act as a policeman and snoop around looking for mistakes, you will find plenty. The more heavy-handed you are in seeking to correct such mistakes, the more unhappy your people will be, the less popular you will be, and the less the objectives of your organisation are likely to be met. And the more the harpies from HQ are likely to start hanging over your head.

As with all things in Thailand so with management, the middle path is usually the best. It is in the nature of the manager beast to keep both eyes open yet turn a blind eye when appropriate. Employ this peculiar vocational trait to the full. Use both eyes, open, to look for what is particularly well done and praise it. Use one eye, closed, to overlook the one flaw in ninety nine perfect pieces.

If the mistakes are not so insignificant that you can happily forget them, then forgive them. Forgive them immediately. Then, privately, enlist the help of the mistake-maker to rectify the situation. Having rectified, he has learnt. Praise him for his good work in remedying the situation and you can walk away like the god of grace. Both of you will feel a lot better.

Punishment for genuine mistakes (not to be confused with dishonesty or sabotage), even if they cost a lot of money, is quite out of place and serves no productive purpose. The shame of having made a mistake is punishment enough. Instead of rubbing the mistake-maker's face in his shame, you should be concerned to make him feel better. Nobody, particularly a Thai, can work well under the shadow of shame.

# NAMES

Thais use first names or nicknames and extend this habit to expats. These names are preceded by a title, usually *Khun*. Learn the names of your staff and use them.

All Thais have two legal names. A personal name which comes first and a family name which comes last. Here the similarities with English end. People will be introduced to you, or introduce themselves, by the first name only, however important they are and however famous the family name.

You can know your staff for years and never have reason to refer to their family names outside of official correspondence. Most expat managers either never learn or quickly forget the family names of their staff. Never mind. It doesn't matter to anybody. And since there are as many Thai family names as there are families (writ large), and most are long, not remembering them is a reasonable use of a manager's time. You might, out of curiosity, look through a list of surnames represented on your staff to see, with the help of your confidential comprador, if any are from the top four or five hundred families, and to see who on your staff are in some way related. You might get some surprises on both counts.

The first name should always be preceded by *Khun*, the equivalent of Mr, Mrs or Miss, unless the bearer is entitled to the honorific *Tahn* (reserved for monks, important government servants and dignitaries, and used more liberally in speeches) or a specific royal, civil service or military title (see TITLES). Businessmen are often referred to as *Nai*, which has more to it than *Khun* but less to it than *Tahn*. Whether speaking in Thai or in English, it is normal to use the polite formula title + first name. Thus, you will find yourself called *Khun* Anne or *Nai* Peter or *Misater*, from the English Mister, Fred or *Dokter* (Doctor) Robert.

Most foreigners like this first name habit. Be aware however that for Thais this is a polite and formal convention. Use of first names conveys none of the implication of friendliness or familiarity that it does in the West.

A number of young Thais, aware of European speech habits, are unwittingly sowing confusion into the name game by referring to foreigners by surname, preceded of course by *Khun*. Motivations are probably good and the individuals are no doubt trying to show respect to the foreigner by correct cultural use of English (although the addition of the Thai word *Khun*, much more frequently heard than Misater, makes it at best half correct). If you like things this way, fine, but you still have to refer to Thais by their first names. If you do not like being the only person referred to by surname, it should be enough for you to point out to your Thai staff that to avoid the confusion of being known by two different names, you would prefer everybody to use your first.

Married women, as married men, are addressed by their first names. Thus the wife of Khun Somboon is *not* Mrs Somboon. Women often, but not always, take the husband's surname, but they are *always* known by their own first names.

You will never learn all Thai first names. There are simply too many of them. Some are common but many are almost unique. Fortunately, it is quite in order to refer to somebody by the easy to say *Khun*, without any name appended, in much the same way as the French use *Monsieur* or *Madame*. However, it sounds strange to use *Khun* without a person's name when talking in English and use is best retained for catching attention (when, strictly speaking, the polite suffix *Khrap* or *Kha* should be added). The English *you*, not polite for catching attention, although *tuk-tuk* drivers have yet to grasp this sensitive point, does a much better job in any conversation.

Thai formal names, the ones on birth certificates and salary slips, can present you with difficulties. Thai nicknames are much easier. Fortunately almost everybody has one.

Almost all nicknames have only one syllable; proper names have two, three or four syllables. There are also fewer nicknames and most mean something in Thai instead of Sanskrit, so you can add to your Thai vocabulary while learning names. What you add will, however, not necessarily help you much in business, unless you are into farming, since nicknames often translate into something that does not sound too flattering in English. Enough said perhaps that the Thai beauty crowned Miss Universe and known overseas as Porntip, is most frequently referred to in Thailand as Khun Pui, which translates as Miss Fertiliser. A rose by any other name would indeed smell as sweet.

If you find somebody's formal name presents difficulties, feel free to ask if he or she has a nickname and free to use it. The fact that you are calling some of your staff by rather earthy Thai nicknames which translate as frog, rat, pig, fatty, shorty and so on, and others by formal, poetic, Sanskrit names, matters not one jot, as long as you remember to put *Khun* before the name. Only close friends and angry enemies would drop the *Khun*, and you are neither.

In Thailand as elsewhere, people like to feel that the boss is taking a personal interest in their welfare. So a little bit of time coming to grips with names or nicknames and using them when talking to your staff will pay dividends.

Nobody expects or particularly wants you to be the chummy boss, but there is little place in Thailand for the amorphous manager who cannot even remember the names of those doing the work for him.

# NEPOTISM

Understand the social obligations of your staff to support their relatives and neither accept nor reject advice simply because it is influenced by nepotism.

Nepotism, the favouring of family members over strangers, is a very natural thing in any country, particularly perhaps in one with a predominantly agricultural economy. Managers, both Thai and expat, must be aware of its possible negative effects on appointments, promotions, and selection of contract tenders. At the same time, they must be aware that any strong attempt to stamp it out might seriously disturb the work place and retard the development of team spirit. The trick is to allow nepotism where it would help create or maintain a working community and avoid nepotism where it would risk adverse reaction on staff morale or productivity.

Be prepared to compromise on the Western tendency to view all nepotism as negative. Nepotism can be seen as an attempt to recreate something of the rural ideal, where economic and social relations are not separated as distinctly as they often are in an urban environment and where a natural and secure life is spent more in the company of trusted family members rather than complete strangers. Do not, in your willingness to compromise, go to the opposite extreme and see recreation of the rural ideal as the objective of managerial activity. After all, you have a business to run and profits to make, and rural ideals are not always suitable for the urban work place.

If your sales manager passes over better qualified and more experienced applicants and wishes to give the assistant sales manager's job to his nephew, he might get a very good assistant he can trust. However, if he knows that his nephew is lazy, none too intelligent and would do the job badly, your sales manager is still likely to feel some obligation to support his relative's application, at least publicly, although perhaps without full enthusiasm. Here it falls to you to sort things out and take full responsibility for appointment. By no means an easy task. But this is one of the advantages of having a expat boss, who is presumably free of social pressures to place personal relationships before questions of productivity. At least, until he marries a Thai.

# OCCASIONS

Special occasions occur so frequently that you will not be able to attend them all, even if you wanted to do so. For many, there is no obligation to attend in person and you can let your money speak for you.

The Thai work world abounds with special occasions. Many an expat manager of a large concern feels that there are too many occasions, each of which requires his time, involvement and money. We will look briefly at a few of the most obvious: New Year, weddings, births, birthdays, promotions and separations, ordinations and funerals.

New Year, the 1 January one, not the Chinese one at the beginning of February, and not the Thai one, 13-15 April, is the one occasion you will find it very difficult to escape. In addition to the formal holiday, resign yourself to losing one day for an extremely long lunch party and expect several of your most social staff (the ones who always get involved in these things) to be far too busy arranging menus, entertainment, games and prizes to think about work for several days beforehand. Before the big day of the party, there will be ritual exchanges of small gifts between office staff in close working contact. For you, it could be difficult to know what to give and where to draw the line.

In the totally Thai world, it would be quite normal for the inferiors to present offerings, together with wishes for the year ahead, to the boss and receive no presents in return. However, you work in an adaptation of that world and can give as well as receive. Distribute presents to those who work directly for you. Nothing too grand or you might embarrass the recipient and set a precedent that you will regret later. On the other hand it could be embarrassing to both parties if your secretary gives you something obviously worth more than you gave her. If this inadvertently happens, nobody mentions it and you follow up with a nice box of chocolates for her children.

If managing a large enterprise, you cannot and need not give new year presents to everybody in your organisation and you certainly do not want to encourage return gifts on such a scale. Quite acceptable is for you, using company money or your own, to give them all a good lunch, certainly with a speech of appreciation. If you can manage it, include a raffle with unwrapped bottles of whisky or other functional items as prizes.

If one of your staff is getting married, you will undoubtedly receive an invitation. Attend if you wish. If, on the other hand, you have already gone through two weddings in one month, have no special feelings for either bride or groom, and would much prefer to spend your Saturday in bed or playing with the children, feel no obligation at all to attend. The obligation is limited to giving a present.

Wedding presents are not quite the same concept in Thailand and in the West. In the West, they assist a couple in setting up home: in Thailand, where a couple might move in with the wife's parents for several years, priority consideration is given to defraying the bride price and considerable expenses of the wedding ceremony and feast. No need to go out and buy a toaster. It would be accepted but is not likely to be conspicuously placed on show as are all the envelopes containing money. Money is the thing. Place an amount, generous enough that no other individual of lesser social standing is likely to give more, in an envelope clearly marked with your name and give it to the person getting married. Alternatively, send it along with somebody you know is going. At the appropriate time in the ceremony, your envelope will be handed over on your behalf.

Not going to *any* of the invitations you receive is most unlikely to result in any sour feelings. In a large enterprise it would probably be impossible to attend every event to which you are invited. In a very small enterprise, or within your unit of a larger one, where you are in daily contact with the inviter, there is more of a social commitment to attend. Obligation is still not there. But if you avoid all such invitations, you could find yourself taking part in little social interaction with your staff. Do not complain that the Thais never invite you for dinner. Inviting *everybody* whenever there is an occasion is the Thai equivalent. Most of your staff will accept such invitations and such coming together for reasons other than work greatly assists social harmony within the work place.

When people are not busy getting married, they are having babies. Gifts for babies are more what you are used to. Clothing or practical items are usual. These may be given if and when you choose to visit mother and baby or during the ceremony or following party held thirty days after birth. Today, not everybody in Bangkok holds this ceremony, so you can really give, or simply send along, your gift whenever you like within a reasonable time after birth.

Birthdays for Thais are, strictly speaking, occasions when the person having the birthday is supposed to treat his friends and workmates rather than receive presents. However, things are changing very fast. It remains usual for the birthday person to invite for a meal at his home, or give a small party in the office. Nobody will object to receiving a small present, not money this time, from the boss. Be aware that for Thais the completion of twelve year cycles marks significant stages in life and birthdays of those aged 12, 24, 36, 48 and 60 are special and involve special celebrations, particularly the sixtieth birthday which traditionally marks a withdrawal from the world.

Clearly work-related occasions such as promotion, retirement and posting to the head office require your involvement to the extent of a speech praising the celebrant and a party within the office of a grandeur to fit status. Very much the same as things back home.

Occasions unlike those back home are those related to the Buddhist religion, principally ordination into the monkhood and cremation. You give money but you are in no sense of the term making a gift. Indeed, the opposite is true and you are using the occasion to *tham boon*: to make religious merit. Whether or not you go to the ordination or the cremation, you can hand over money in an envelope with a request to be allowed to *tham boon*.

On all of the occasions involving gifts or contributions of a personal nature and unsolicited by the receiver, expect no acknowledgment of your generosity. (See GIFTS.) In contrast, solicited donations are given great fanfare. Be warned that a request for money to repair a temple roof, sponsor an event at a school sports day or give to a fund for this year's disaster can produce results different to those in the West. The altruistic business giver in the West might place a small amount anonymously in an envelope. The less altruistic might write out a cheque for a much larger, tax-deductible amount. Whatever the amount or motive, however, unless he is doing things in a very big way, such as setting up a foundation or scholarship with his name immortalised in the title, he does not expect his gift to receive publicity. In Thailand, the precise size of your donation is likely to be publicised in the press, through duplicated circulars, or over a loudspeaker system, together with your name and the name of your company. Such public acclaim of the value of your gift might seem somewhat vulgar to Western ways of thinking.

A final word on occasions which are hard to ignore. These are invitations by big men or Thai business partners. There might or might not be something to celebrate. Your wife might be invited if somebody happens to think of it.

Such occasions always start with an expensive dinner in a restaurant. Usually there will be entertainment provided. It is quite normal for men to show their appreciation by publicly handing over banknotes, with or

without a garland of flowers, to a singer or dancer. This does not, or should not, indicate any expectation of return favours. It also happens sometimes that individuals are called from the audience to come forward and show their appreciation. Nobody wants a speech from you expressing your delight in the young lady's mastery of song. Just give the money, with or without an envelope, and return to your seat quickly to explain to your wife, if she has decided it is safer to come along and keep an eye on you, that it is all just a harmless bit of fun and that really you have never seen the girl before in your life.

# OPPOSING VIEWS

Critical expression of differences of opinion is
carefully avoided. Resolution of conflicting points
of view is less a matter of dialectical debate than of
behind the scenes management.

In the West, differences of opinion are something to be
aired. This is considered a much healthier and more
productive state of affairs than hiding differences away or
pretending they don't exist.

By extension of reasoning, just about everything must
have two or more different views. Therefore, on the rare
occasions when a spontaneous critical opposition is lacking,

one person may deliberately take the role of devil's advocate, setting out the other side of the coin to prompt discussion and ensure that everything has been considered that should be considered. A synthesis of opposing views or a choice between two or more alternatives would be made when all facts and viewpoints have been clearly stated.

In Thailand, differences of opinion exist but critical expression of these differences is carefully avoided. Resolution of conflicting points of view is less a matter of dialectical debate than of behind the scenes manipulation.

Open, public statement of opposing views is usually limited to the ultra-critical statements of the kind one politician makes of another in the media. This is tantamount to an act of war; hopefully of the cold rather than the hot type, but likely to cause long lasting bitterness and most certainly not likely to be activated by a wish to consider all points of view. Such opposition does not take place within a group unless it is splitting up or being sabotaged by a member who has decided to attach himself to a patron in a contending faction.

What is the expat manager to do? Well, having seen what happens when Thais fall out, you clearly must think very carefully before encouraging dialectical debate. Perhaps it is better to put your efforts and time into seeing staff individually, to pick their brains quietly before *you* decide between alternatives. If you have a nice, harmonious set up, why look for an antithesis?

# PROBLEM SHARING

Problems are shared in one direction only, upwards
with somebody of greater knowledge or influence,
and for reasons as often related to the pragmatic
(solving) as the psychological (coping).

A problem shared is a problem halved. Maybe. But this
particular adage is not known in Thailand. Problems are
shared, often with the hope of resolving them, but not
quite in the same way that many expat managers would be
used to back home. In Thailand, sharing is not likely to
involve equals, to have no element of direct reciprocity in
the sense of talking through each other's problems, and to
be directed more at resolution than at psychological
assistance in coping with problems you are stuck with.

Problems are shared in the sense of enlisting the help
of somebody to solve or reduce them. The person
approached for help will be more knowledgable or more
influential than the person doing the approaching. All
logical enough: what is the point in expecting help from
someone who knows less and can pull fewer strings? So
you only share your problems with somebody more
important than you and you would expect only those less
important than you to ask for your help with their problems.
The same is true for problems purely work related and for
personal problems. Of course, all the norms of respect

inherent in Thai social structure come into play.

This does not mean that your social inferiors in the office cannot help you to solve work-related problems. Do not hesitate to ask the computer man to run through all payments received this year and try to account for a missing sum of money. He is only doing his job and you are simply doing your job. If, however, the missing sum is substantial and is owed by an influential person, you might rightly be said to have a problem, and one that is not likely to be solved by gathering your subordinates together to brainstorm the situation. You have got to look upwards for your help. By all means pray to God and make offerings to the Buddha, but perhaps you can find material assistance at a somewhat lower level of authority.

If you want help from those above, it is only fair and reasonable that you be prepared to help out those on your staff who might come to you with their problems. This is the Thai way of obtaining reciprocity.

Do not be surprised if your respectful staff member seems to want to talk about matters which have little relationship to the world of work. If your accounts clerk wants to tell you how bad she is feeling these days because her best friend, who you do not know and never will, has committed suicide, hide your embarrassment and be a good listener.

It is not usual for a Thai to burden a friend with her or his personal problems. It is more usual to keep personal feelings to oneself and to suffer in silence. The acceptable exception is to tell problems to a respected authority figure. Often a monk, sometimes a wise person with a reputation for giving good advice and lending a sympathetic ear, perhaps a professional *mor duu* (a seer), and perhaps a pleasant boss. It will not happen every day and, depending on your character, might not happen to you at all. But if it does, take it as a sign of respect. If you have no practical suggestions for dealing with the problem, a few words of sympathy will help your staff member. It will also confirm that you care about your people. Which is as it should be.

Problem sharing is a one-way communication. You listen but you definitely do not tell your problems in return. Some of the problems which come the way of your ears only might well be work related. Thais are human and have their likes and dislikes, their secret loves and their deep hatreds. They will hide them publicly much better than many non-Thais; however, if somebody does come to you with a virulent attack against a colleague, it portends trouble and must be taken seriously.

A complaint against a fellow worker might have brewed in the mind for a long time and be difficult to put into words. Therefore it might seem to you to lack any clear base on which you can act. As manager, this is not really the time for a sympathetic ear. Action is required. If two people do not get on, do *not* have them both in to sort things out. If ways can be found so that the two do not come into contact, that might be the best solution. If, on the other hand, their work depends on interaction, you might have no choice but to spend some time with the complaining staff member to point out the importance of working together with the hated partner. And at least trying to get to the cause of the problem.

If the cause of the conflict becomes obvious, the solution might also be obvious. As likely as not, however, it will remain hidden. If both parties like you, and if you make it clear to each independently, without criticism of either, that you depend on their working well together, there is just a chance that they might settle or suppress differences, at least for a time.

You should listen when somebody brings a problem to you but you have no obligation to solve it in that person's interests. The big man to whom you take your problem might feel the same way, particularly if your problem involves another person who has already demonstrated personal loyalty. A good reason for you and your comprador to keep your genteel spy network well honed and another reason for not wearing your heart and your problems on your sleeve.

# QUIET

Thais seem to possess an ability to work in the noisiest of settings. But a raised voice is to be avoided and will damage communications.

Mention the noise level in the world beyond the enclosed, double glazed, air-cocooned office to most Thais and they will agree with you and wonder what on earth you are talking about. It seems to many an expat that the Thais are born with an extraordinary ability not to see whatever they don't want to see and not to hear whatever they don't want to hear. The expat manager or businessman does not have to fear unduly that noise levels that might break some industrial code back home will affect the ability of the Thai worker to churn out the product.

This capacity to turn off and ignore almost any noise, does not mean that a Thai will ignore a raised voice. Whatever you have to say should be said quietly. Even the big man should not really talk any louder than polite conversation requires. The more humble you are, the quieter you should be. If you are really very humble indeed, you should probably not be heard at all. This provides you with a nice explanation of why the little girl who empties your waste bin and out tray is afraid to speak to you in any language.

All this politeness does not help communication. The language barrier is enough of a problem without having to read lips. If you suspect that somebody has not fully understood you, and the chances are always that he has not, then repeat yourself and try using different words and sentence patterns, but do not raise your voice. There is a natural tendency to do this.

To a Thai, a loud voice means anger and the threat of punishment. This is not what you want to communicate at all and it could stop your real message getting through. To get minds working on trying to understand what you mean, speak quietly.

# RELIGION

Predominantly Buddhist, Thailand is very tolerant
of its religious minorities, all of which have their
special days and activities. Religious activity
remains very evident in the work place and can
help the manager promote a working community.

The population of Thailand is some 90% Buddhist, with
significant Muslim and Christian minorities and smaller
numbers of Hindus, Sikhs, Taoists and what are usually
referred to as animists, meaning belief in a wide variety of
spirits, often coupled with ancestor worship. Things are
not always clear-cut and centuries of religious tolerance
have developed a syncretic view of religion.

Most people classify themselves as Buddhists and take
part in Buddhistic ceremonies and celebrations, some of
which are national holidays. They also make offerings to
Hindu deities, particularly the elephant god, and maintain,
at all levels of the social structure, beliefs, customs,
ceremonies and festivals which are Hindu in origin. Many
Christians, Hindus, Taoists, and Sikhs similarly feel they
can accept all or part of the teachings of the Lord Buddha
without compromising their specific religious beliefs and
many will take part openly in Buddhist ceremony.
Whatever the religion, just about everybody has some
belief in spirits (see VOWS) and some elements of religious

practice that could be interpreted as ancestor worship.

The Muslim population is a majority in the southernmost provinces, where most people are ethnically Malay and speak a Malay dialect at home. There is also a significant Muslim representation in Bangkok and you should not be at all surprised to find that some of your staff members are Muslim. They will speak Thai and look Thai but will have religious practices that other Thais do not share. The most significant of these for you to bear in mind relate to the Muslim taboo against eating pork and the annual maintenance of the month of Ramadan, which varies each year. In large enterprises a concession is often given to a small Muslim caterer, whose food will also be welcomed by Buddhist Thais, to supplement the main canteen services. During Ramadan, Muslims can work but should not eat, drink or smoke during daylight hours. At this time, it is reasonable to allow some flexibility in working hours and to permit Muslim staff members to take leave during the month and particularly at the end of it, which is marked by a large feast.

Many Christians are also ethnic Chinese. However, it is difficult to say just who is Chinese and who is Thai and it is also sometimes difficult to say with precision what is Christian. Christian Thais often follow Buddhist and/or Taoist rites for their dead parents and most Buddhist Thais in Bangkok are happy enough to celebrate Christmas. Christmas is not a holiday in Thailand, but the expat manager will no doubt sympathise with Christian staff members who wish to take the day off.

The number of Christians on the staff of international

companies is probably more than proportionate to representation throughout the country; because of the association of American missionaries with a number of Thai churches and schools, many speak good English.

Modernisation seems to pose no great threat to Buddhism, which thrives as well in the office and workshop as in the rice fields. Everywhere, you will see material signs of belief. On the top of the filing cabinet next to the secretary, you will see pictures of her family next to pictures of a particularly revered monk, pictures of the Royal Family and probably a picture of King Chulalongkorn the Great. All can be regarded, for your practical purposes, as sacred. In the bank, you will notice a Buddha image on a shelf on the wall. In the office of your Thai partner or government contact you might see several tiers of Buddha images with offerings of flowers and incense. Smaller images are worn around the neck or kept at a respectful height.

The office minibus is festooned with flower garlands and images of Buddhas and monks at the front. The entire office staff will sign up for the annual office visit to a distant temple to make Khatin offerings. Whenever you pass the spirit house on the company's grounds, you will see your people making offerings and saying prayers. Traditional religious practices are very much alive. The modern workplace has not detracted from Buddhism; it might be more true to say that it has been adapted to serve the religious needs of your staff. The prevalence of religious symbols and activities help a great deal in forging a working community and you should appreciate that tradition is on your side in this important managerial objective.

# STRESS

Life and work in Thailand is not all a bed of lotus flowers and Thais are by no means immune to stress. Principal causes of stress for your staff apart from the difficulties of life in Bangkok can be management related: jealousy of colleagues, rushing to meet deadlines, isolation, disturbances to happy routine and, most of all, criticism.

Thai society is structured on a status hierarchy which accommodates without encouraging individual mobility and provides everybody with both a very clear idea of his or her place and a code of appropriate social interaction. To put this another way, people are kept together by being kept apart. The whole structure of superficially relaxed but correct social relationships is held up by a mild tension of aggression avoidance through internalisation of feelings. Or to put that another way: stress.

Stress is as much a part of Thai personality as is sensitivity, charm, tolerance and beauty. Breach sensitivities by unreasonable demands or criticism and you increase stress beyond the point where it is functional. Functional stress means a person is not totally relaxed; he is neither deep in meditation nor is he asleep, he is awake and alert and not preoccupied with nasty thoughts. He can interact with other people and can work. This is the level of stress that you should aim at, for yourself and for your staff.

Any work as a boss is going to involve stress. Probably more for a boss bossing outside of his own country. And any work as the bossed is also going to involve stress. Probably more if the boss is a foreigner and outside of the known code of social interaction. Let's look, as good managers should, from the worker's point of view.

A primary source of stress, particularly for those fresh from the rice fields, is the urban environment of Bangkok. Not much you, or for that matter the Bangkok municipal authorities, can do about that. But you can recognise that your tensions, built up by driving through the jams in a comfortable air-conned car with soothing music of your choice to a comfortable home, might be envied by those of your staff who have no choice other than to hang on a crowded bus for long distances as likely as not with competing volumes of traffic noise and the bus driver's choice of far from soothing music to a home that possesses less creature comforts than it does creatures. How do they put up with it and still arrive at the office clean and smart and smiling?

Take a ride on a bus yourself and look at the faces. Nobody complaining, no facial contortions indicative of torture, no pushing and shoving and no telling the bus boy where to put his phallic money box. Almost everybody is practising the fine art of withdrawal. Calm faces. Not happy, just withdrawn from the experience. An admirable way to prevent a Bangkok bus causing permanent damage to the psyche, but not a complete escape from the stress of urban life and certainly not the best way to cope with the tortures of typing your memo's to Head Office.

The second source of stress for your staff is likely to be you, particularly if you have just arrived. You will understandably feel a strong tendency to come to grips with your new job and show what everybody knows anyway, that you are the boss. At the very moment when you have what seems to be a million personal things to do before you and your family can feel settled, you might well consider that you have little choice other than to put in long hours at the office, especially if you have a short overlap period with your predecessor, who is himself as likely as not a bundle of nerves trying to fit all the goodbyes into the space between packing and selling off his assets.

If you have a choice, and usually there is one, decide that for a certain period, let's say at least two weeks, you are going to make no significant work decisions and will spend most of your time getting to know your staff and sorting out your personal life. The two activities are easily combined in Thailand. Your people will be only too willing to advise you on getting a house or flat, showing you where to buy furniture and perhaps helping you to find servants. Getting to know at least some of your staff in this practical way is infinitely better than trying to meet everybody at once in an office full of infectious nervous tension.

Just as you are at your most vulnerable on arrival, so a Thai entering your enterprise is at most risk of stress, particularly if he or she has never worked for a foreigner before. Somebody among your staff will quickly befriend the newcomer and guide him into a supportive social group. You, as the boss, cannot be that friend, but you should spend at least some time with the person to show that you are reasonable and human. (And you are, otherwise you would not have got this far in this book.)

The new arrival will naturally feel on probation and be more concerned with demonstrating capacity to do the work than with getting to know the work. If he has moved into Bangkok in order to take up the job, let him know that you expect him to take some time off to get the kids into school and so on. Certainly do not pick this time to lay down the law; the "law" should have been evident at the hiring stage. Unless you have serious doubts about the newcomer, make it clear as soon as you reasonably can that the probationary period is now over.

On to some sources of stress where Thai ways of seeing might not completely coincide with the ways you look at things back home. The great bogey of CRITICISM has been covered under that section: fair or not, criticism will cause stress. Privacy is another concept open to different cultural interpretation. The Good Management Manual states *Privacy is essential to mental peace and good work*. In the West, encroachment on personal space can be a source of resentment. In Thailand, working alongside another person is more likely to be a source of welcome company, and if personal space implies isolation, it could increase rather than reduce stress. However, let's be careful with these generalisations. Your high status staff will certainly not be happy if status space is ignored. The bigger the man, the bigger the office. Actual space is not as important as comparative space. True anywhere in the world. Especially so in status-conscious Thailand.

A cause of stress rare in Thailand is the over-ambitious staff member. Ambition is certainly less naked than in the West, but exceptions do sometimes crop up. In the West the overly ambitious feed on each other, in Thailand they tend to feed on more passive colleagues. Just one of these exceptional people in your office can offend the sensitivities of your entire staff. Since the exceptional is quite probably an unsackable daughter of a general you must proceed tactfully if you wish to avoid generating even more stress. You might consider advising such a person that the opportunities for her (his) talents on offer within the company are so limited that you cannot do her justice and since the director of (introduce the name of your main competitor) is looking for just such a person to occupy a senior position, you would be prepared, in the staff member's own interest, to put in a very good word for her for this chance in a lifetime.

While your staff is unlikely to be over-ambitious, all of them will expect regular and fair promotion. If it appears that the younger, more attractive or more charming, who perhaps speak better English and get on well with the boss, get ahead too fast, it can cause resentment, perhaps a feeling of inadequacy, and stress for those left behind.

All changes at work can affect the level of stress. In the West there is much talk of job enrichment to prevent boredom and provide more sense of accomplishment. If you have a staff member who strikes you as one who would appreciate some enrichment, go ahead. As long as it does not disturb the more routine tempo of the work place. For most of your staff, you might be better advised to look from a different direction. If they are happy with things the way they are and work all right, changing work tasks is likely to increase nothing but stress. If you do feel the need to make changes, bear in mind that, in Thailand particularly, giving a person work to do for which he is not trained, not intellectually equipped or not physically able will not make him rise to the challenge but rapidly sink under shame and stress.

Another cause of stress is deadlines and constant urging to hurry up. Many Thais can remain productive for prolonged periods as long as things are steady, sure and agreeable, but fall apart when they are rushed. Hurrying creates stress. Most deadlines follow cycles and, with a little thought, you can work most of them into the monthly or annual routine, avoiding the panic of crisis management.

The symptoms of stress shown by your Thai staff might initially be none too evident and could lead you into a false complacency that everything is going fine. Individual or collective stress can be hidden behind the mask and internalised for a long time. Early warning signs might be limited to the kind of withdrawal evident on the faces of Bangkok bus passengers. Some such volcanoes remain forever dormant. Others suddenly erupt.

You can start to reduce the stress level among your staff by limiting your own exposure to stress producing activities. Manage your time by cutting down on the number and length of meetings (see MEETINGS) and limit your exposure to social functions, which might be relaxing for a

Thai but can be a source of stress for the foreigner: a language you can't understand, food you can't eat, being always on display, expected to give speeches at the drop of a chopstick and under the constant fear of making social gaffs. If you feel stress, so will your staff. A long face is enough to turn people away from you. Your image may be but superficial but it is important and cannot be separated from your personal mood. Everybody finds it easier to relax with a cheerful boss. Thus, to a degree, you can reduce stress simply by smiling. The old adage one smile makes two is particularly appropriate in Thailand.

# STRIKES

Thai reluctance to enter into a conflict situation means that when a complaint is made, there is almost always a good reason for it.

Strikes in Thailand rarely take on the magnitude of industrial conflict in the West, generally receive little coordinated support and are over quite quickly. This has less to do with cultural aspects of business in Thailand than it has to do with the level of trade union development and the existence of a legal code which could be said to favour employers. It is relevant, however, that in spite of a strongly felt need to go along with group decisions, the average Thai worker would much prefer to avoid conflict before resorting to attempts at conflict resolution through industrial action.

Group action is likely to be preceded by attempts to remedy real or imagined wrongs by means less likely to result in loss of face for either side. Strikes are almost unknown among foreign enterprises established in Thailand because pay and conditions are often better than in some of the less well controlled companies which fail to maintain legal requirements.

Conflicts with which you might come into contact are likely to have a built-in compromise readily discernible and to take the form of a request rather than an ultimatum.

One traditional mechanism occasionally used on the industrial front is the petition. This will be signed by all the workers or by their representatives and directed to the highest point of management within Thailand. It will outline the problem faced by the workforce, or part of it, and request assistance from the respected big man or men. If you handle it well, you will meet the representatives, probably several times, and they will understand if you need time to get back to Headquarters. Pleasant meetings taking time will help the spirit of compromise develop and some bosses manage to come out of such a situation with no loss of face and their position positively enhanced because they have demonstrated that, although not everything requested can be given, they know how to look after their people.

Thai reluctance to enter into a conflict situation means that when a complaint is made, there is almost always some good reason for it. Occasionally, the request/complaint might seem somewhat bizarre. If workers are worried by an unreasonable and unexplained incidence of bad luck or sickness among the labour force and want a spirit house built and offerings made, do not hesitate to do it. After you have done it, look for any more rational industrial reason for the misfortunes. If asbestos is falling from the ceiling, construction of a spirit house might temporarily placate the workers but it is unlikely to solve the problem.

However politely couched, expressions of dissatisfaction should always be given very serious consideration. If they are, the smiles will come back and any possibility of a strike or other serious industrial action will fade away.

# TELEPHONES

In a city as logistically problematic as Bangkok, the telephone is likely to be necessary to obtain those initial important meetings. But until people have met and developed a degree of trust, nothing very significant is likely to get said over the telephone.

Face to face communication in Thailand is accompanied by sometimes obvious and sometimes very subtle signals of respect that are given out with every word or movement, or silence and non-movement. These signals are not so evident on the telephone, where a tendency towards verbal over-compensation often gives the impression that one of the partners in the communication has a vocabulary limited to one word, *khrap* (man speaking) and *kha* (woman speaking). These words are no more or less than particles of speech indicating respect (they can often be translated as *yes* or *I agree*).

Requesting a meeting with an outside big man is best done over the telephone from your secretary to his. You, not he, will brave the traffic at whatever time is convenient to him. If the superior is out of town, you wait until he might be back in town and try again. If he is then at a conference in Pattaya, you might suggest a meeting between your deputy and his. Nothing would be decided at such a meeting, since delegation of responsibility for anything more than the most trivial of matters is rare. The big man would, however, get more of an idea of what you want than a secretary can convey on the telephone and could decide to see you. If so, his secretary will call you. Rush on over. If he calls you back personally and wants to talk on the 'phone, perhaps he is not as big as you thought he was. Or perhaps he thinks you are more important than you are. If there is a real understanding of near equality between you, very good, but take care all the same. Both of you should be very polite. Rarely would anything significant get said over the telephone until people have met and developed a degree of trust.

# TICKING OFF

Pointing out that somebody is doing something wrongly is a form of criticism and should be avoided if alternatives are possible. If there is no alternative, get your timing right, make use of the status structure and play by the ground rules.

However much you praise your staff, gain popularity and have a happy workplace, there will inevitably come times when you have to point out that somebody is doing something wrongly or that their performance is not all it could be.

If an alternative to ticking off exists, use it. Many minor corrections to the performance of work tasks can be handled by providing information on *new* procedures and by suggestion rather than criticism. Introducing something as new fully disguises any critical element and prevents loss of face. Camouflaging orders as what-if suggestions creates opportunities for errant staff members to confirm their agreement, support and loyalty.

If you can think of ways round the critical telling off which get your message across without making people dislike you, so much the better. If not, it is important that you remain in full control of the reprimand. To ensure that you are in full control of yourself and the situation, timing is important.

Views on appropriate timing might not be quite the same for Thai and expatriate managers. In the West, an employee is ticked off as soon as his misdeed is discovered. The crime is fresh, the punishment given and hopefully all can then get down to work. In Thailand, the boss picks the time. Never when angry. Let the offending staff member sweat, not you. If he comes to you to apologise, accept in good grace.

If there is no spontaneous admission of guilt, wait until you have the time and are in a reasonable mood. Circle in to the subject. Ask a few questions of a personal nature which would probably draw the response *mind your own bloody business* back in Islington but which, in Thailand, would reinforce the correct relationship between boss-patron and worker-client. You show interest in the welfare of a subordinate; he or she responds with loyalty and obedience.

For more serious or repeated offences. Make a clear point of seeing the guilty one. Alone, of course. Being called to the boss's office is already a warning that something is wrong. In the good old days, a wrongdoer might have been kept waiting to reflect on his sins for several weeks before quakingly crawling in. Today, when people are actually getting paid and offices have lost their grandiose antechambers, this might be regarded by HQ as mismanagement of time and space. Even so, a studied minute before looking up from your papers and granting permission to enter should make the tone of the meeting clear enough without saying a word.

Quietly, when you feel the moment has come, and assuming there has been no pre-emptive admission of guilt in the hope of cutting punishment by 50%, you will have to mention clearly the reason for your summons. If you get a statement which somehow promises that things will get better and not worse, change the subject and try to end on a pleasant note. There is nothing worse than a boss who goes on and on, deliberately making the person squirm and apologise *ad nauseam*. Now is the time for the paternalistic approach and a reaffirmation that you value and look after good workers.

If you fail to receive the *mea culpa*, you will have to give more authority, not more explanation, to your reasons. Throwing your weight behind the ticking off means dropping the important indirect aspect of criticism. It might work in the specific instance but you could lose out in the popularity stakes and therefore risk longer term negative results. There is another way which might just leave you as clean and loved as you began.

It sometimes helps to become once removed from the source of authority. Everybody has superiors. Yours might be more of a nuisance than a help, particularly if completely out of touch with the realities of your situation, sitting in London, Geneva or New York passing cryptic comments on your monthly reports. Why not make those guys do some work for a change, even if they don't know they are doing it? What could be more fun than making them unwittingly work for you? If the situation requires it, which it does if there is any risk to your personal popularity, bring the whole weight of the system to your assistance. If your Thai staff member screws up, *you* are going to be held responsible by the big men at Head Office.

The technique of passing the buck upwards to those who control you all and must be obeyed can only work properly if you are *liked* by the person being indirectly criticised. If you are not liked, nobody will care if you get into trouble. So, having agreed between you to a course of action which will keep the big shots from trampling all your heads into the dirt, don't forget to send the cause of all your trouble a couple of creamy cakes to sweeten the aftermath of the ticking off.

Ticking sensitive people off is a subtle art and the same format cannot be followed every time. The following basic ground rules should act as a guide.

162

1  Avoid public confrontation at all costs.
2  See the person yourself.
3  Pick the best time. Never when you are angry.
4  Try to balance criticism with praise.
5  Be indirect and offer suggestions rather than criticisms.
6  Be as nice as possible and as popular as possible.

# TITLES

A great many important people have titles: royal, civil service or military. It is essential to use them, particularly on any correspondence.

Royal titles decrease in status and scarcity following a five-generation rule. Any title will almost certainly be displayed in abbreviated form on namecards and invitations and provides an instant guide to status. These titles are never translated, since the ranking system is conceptually different to that in England. They are instead transcribed in English. Correspondence places the abbreviation, whether in Thai or English, before the given name. Royal titles are as follows:

1  P.O.C. – Phra Ong Chao, grandchild of King
2  M.C. – Mom Chao, child of P.O.C.
3  M.R – Mom Rajawong, child of M.C.
4  M.L. – Mom Luang, child or wife of M.R. and wife of M.C.

With the fifth generation the title is lost. The Royal Family stands in a category above all these ranks.

Another set of titles relate to the civil service and remain in frequent use, particularly among the more mature members of the Thai establishment. These are in descending order:

1 Chao Phya (wife: Khun Ying)
2 Phya
3 Phra
4 Luang
5 Khun (in Thai spelt and pronounced differently from Khun meaning "you" or "Mr")

Military ranks are also used in Thailand, as in the West, when the holder has already left the service. Very important politicians have a tendency to hold a high military rank. These ranks are translated into American English. The English equivalent is used in all English communications and the Thai is therefore not given here.

If somebody has a title, use it in place of *you*, *he* or *her* (or the everyday *Khun*), together with the first name, when talking to them or about them.

# UNTOUCHABILITY

Taboos on touching across the sex line extend
fully into the working world and can pose problems
for women. Within sexual boundaries, touching,
including the handshake, is viewed differently by
Thais and non-Thais.

Touching across the sex line is, to all intents and purposes,
taboo in and out of the workplace. Inappropriate contact
by a manager, expat or Thai, is not likely to result in
litigation on charges of sexual harassment or misconduct,
but it will not help your overall popularity and could set
tongues wagging. So, however fatherly you might feel
towards the young lady working on your accounts, do not
put your arm around her shoulders or even one hand upon

one shoulder.

The same warning is magnified for the expat woman working in Thailand or accompanying her husband. Although in many ways you will be regarded as an honorary man when it comes to meetings and cocktail parties, keep your hands to yourself and discourage male hands from even thinking of wandering over in your direction. If you do not you will obtain a reputation hard for you or your husband to live with and harder to live down.

There is one safe exception used between people of either sex in a regular working relationship. It is acceptable, and fairly frequent, for a light touch to be made to the other person's elbow to draw attention. Having read this you will understand if it should happen to you or if you see it around in the office. However, rather than try to perfect practice of the exception, or to factor in changing concepts of propriety and individual tolerances, you are safer simply to regard the opposite sex, at least in the workplace and in public, as untouchable.

Taboos on physical contact do not apply between members of the same sex. A press photograph of the Prime Minister hand in hand with a male colleague would raise no eyebrows at all. Do not be surprised if a Thai you hardly know takes your hand as you file out of a meeting. Probably he has something to say to you, even if it is a simple enquiry as to how things are going. Avoid reading anything significant into the action, it does not necessarily imply solidarity with the application of your company for a license to build a high-rise in a low-rise zone, and it almost certainly is not a prelude for sexual advances. Such behaviour is supposed to set you at ease but, if you are Western, is likely to have the opposite effect. There is no easy way out. An explanation of Western norms seems out of place and might be taken as criticism of Thai ways, whipping your hand away would be seen as an unfriendly act, keeping both hands in your pockets is quite sloppy and anyway would not prevent your arm being taken.

Touching, even within the same sex, can be touchy. A hand on the knee or on the shoulder is all right if the superior is doing the touching or if equals are involved. A slap on the back might be fine between gauchos but will not be well received by Thais. Absolutely out is touching the hair or head, although this is OK for young children.

The touching which comes most naturally to many Westerners is the handshake. Some Thais in regular contact with Americans and Europeans don't seem to mind it. But many find it unnatural and are confused as to correct formality and meaning. Who should put out his hand first, the superior or the inferior? The action smacks too much of social equality for many Thais to feel really comfortable about it. A male expat extending his hand to a Thai woman risks making her feel uncomfortable on both counts, the touching and the implied equality of status. Between men, holding hands poses no problem but shaking hands does.

Some foreigners will not feel happy conducting business without the ritual handshake. Shake on a deal if you must and the Thai is likely to understand and perhaps even appreciate the meaning of the gesture. But the Frenchman who is always shaking appendages would be advised to consider the alternatives available. The smile, the verbal greeting, the nodded head can all be used in place of a handshake for most occasions and can cross the sex line. With a little thought, the Thai *wai* can be added to the list. Of course, if a Thai man, or a Thai woman, holds out a hand towards you, by all means shake it.

# VOWS

The practice of making and keeping vows is endemic among Thais. It provides psychological assistance in times of uncertainty, helps maintain overall harmony and provides an explanation when things go wrong. You should make full use of this cost-effective traditional habit and assist your enterprise by providing a facility for votive behaviour on your premises.

The habit of making vows and keeping them if wishes are fulfilled is widespread among Thais at all social levels. The form and value of the promise made in each case corresponds to the magnitude of the favour asked of the spirit world or of a particular deity. Thus if a request is made for a father to recover from a terminal illness, for a million baht win on the lottery, for promotion from filing clerk to director, or for the expat manager to leave his wife and marry the tea girl, some pretty high stakes are involved. Vows made in connection with the unlikely might involve a barefoot walk across a fire pit, financing the renovation of a temple or living as a monk or nun for a fixed period of time.

Vows, like bribes, are not paid off until the results come in. Therefore nobody has anything to lose by wishing for the moon, and everybody does it at some time. However, people like to have their wishes met most of the time. For this reason most vows are made well within the realm of possibility.

Some people cannot go more than a few days without making some sort of vow. They love the reassurance brought through fulfillment of wishes, however minor, and love the actions involved in keeping vows. Requested favours can be very mundane: that the doctor's prescription will work and a mild infection will disappear, that the house will not be burgled while everybody is away on holiday, that the boss will give a reasonable performance evaluation report. Such vows involve comparatively minor expenses and can be as simple as giving a small wooden elephant to the spirit house on the corner or a supply of flowers and incense. Vows can also serve social functions: family and friends can be invited to help maintain a vow to stick one hundred pieces of gold leaf on the Buddhas of Chachoengsao, to be followed of course by a good lunch.

How to make use of such votive behaviour, as anthropologists call it, for the benefit and smooth running of your enterprise? Well, it certainly does no harm to have the spirits on your side and on the side of your workforce. Since most vows can be made anywhere, there is every reason for providing a facility for making them on workplace premises, which is the logical and convenient place to make and keep vows related to problems at work. This facility takes the form of a spirit house, set up with all due ceremony in one corner of your location, to act as a home for the land spirits you have dispossessed by your modern enterprise.

Offerings will be made at the spirit house by many of your staff, even when no specific vow is involved. For the individuals on your workforce, a rapport with the local spirits provides a rationale to stay put if things are going well, a non-confrontational psychological escape if things are not going so well, and hope for the future. For the company, building a spirit house is probably more effective, and certainly more cost-effective, than bringing in teams of industrial psychologists to study social interaction in the workplace.

# WAI

The *wai* is not a way of saying hello without using words. Misuse can make you look ridiculous. Reason enough to read on.

The *wai* is the most significant of the many social actions that reinforce Thai social structure. It is given full treatment in the opening chapter of the companion volume to this book, *Culture Shock Thailand*. Unfortunately, many expats misuse the *wai* and make themselves look rather ridiculous at the critical moments involved in opening meaningful rapport with their staff and profitable relationships with business contacts.

Think of the *wai* as a respect continuum. The lower the head comes down to meet the thumbs of both hands, pressed palms together and held fingers upwards, the more respect is shown.

Knowing when to *wai* is even more important than knowing how to *wai*. Sometimes the *wai* should *not* be used. The rule here is that when the status difference between any two individuals is very great, the *wai* is not returned. Thus a child greeting an elder, a waitress receiving a tip from a client, a junior employee seeing the big boss, a commoner meeting the King, any layman in audience with any monk, should *wai*. Such a *wai* may be acknowledged with a nod or a smile but it is not returned.

As a general practical guide, feel free to return a *wai* from your office staff, unless it is used to say thank you, as a formality on entering or leaving your office, or when requesting permission to hand something to you. Then a smile is enough. An inappropriate *wai* can embarrass people.

Also feel free to initiate a *wai* with important business or Government contacts. You should get one back. However, people in regular contact do not spend all day *wai*ing each other, once a day is usually enough and sometimes too much.

# WORK AND RICE

Cooperation at work plays an important role in maintaining good social relations and cohesion, whether within a village neighbourhood and within an entire village or within a modern work unit and the entire enterprise of which that unit forms a part.

The gap between life in Bangkok and life in the village is a chasm. But the Bangkok-based manager should remember that the chasm is bridged continuously by fleets of long distance buses careering between the great rice-eating metropolis and the most distant rice-producing villages, carrying many of the members of his workforce home to fulfil social obligations. He should remember also that many of his people are almost as displaced in Bangkok as he is. Like him, they came mainly for the money, much of which goes back home. Most of all he should remember that in the context of Thai society as a whole, the various industries of Bangkok and nearby remain second fiddle to the rice-producing hinterland of upcountry Thailand.

The majority of Thais are rice farmers and rice cultivation is likely to continue to be the most important single economic activity in Thailand for a long time to come. The cultivation of rice ensures subsistence for some 60 million people within national boundaries and provides very significant export earnings. Rice is treated with quasi-religious respect. Farmers in their distant fields and the Monarch in the very centre of the Kingdom take part in ceremonies to promote good harvests. Rice is one of the central elements in national identity and the social and economic patterns of life associated with its cultivation are dominant elements of Thai personality and behaviour. Moving from the farm to the factory involves adjustments, but personality and centuries-old patterns of behaviour do not change overnight. These long established patterns of behaviour, you should be happy to hear, are fully compatible with economic rationality.

Cooperation between rice-producers is not indicative of any tendency towards primitive communism and is rarely prompted by altruistic motives. Far from it. Each person secures maximum economic gains. To paraphrase

what Lenin worked out long ago, scratch a Thai peasant and you will find a little capitalist under the dust.

When economic gains are not intrinsic to cooperation, the organization of work activities is limited to the individual producer and his immediate family. The solitary farmer with his buffalo, whether of the traditional grass-fed animal or of the modern petrol-fed iron variety, is a familiar sight at ploughing time. It would make no sense for a group of villagers to get together with their buffaloes and plough on a cooperative basis. Indeed, such an inappropriate pattern of work organisation would make a hell of a mess of the fields.

Two work tasks call for a labour force larger than most single families can put together: the transplant and the harvest. Cooperation is possible in the transplant because seedlings in one of the various family held nurseries are ready for movement before those in other nurseries. When they are ready to move, they do not like to be kept waiting. They must be uprooted, bundled together and transplanted as rapidly as possible. Three days out of the soil and they are all dead. Cooperation is required for maximum productivity. Much the same rationale explains cooperation at harvest time. One man's rice will mature before another man's.

Deciding whose nurseries or fields should receive priority and the order in which fields should be worked requires knowledge and experience. Certain individuals are likely to be listened to before others. If very large groups are working in cooperation, a village rice committee might be elected. All involved in cooperation would also, in some way, be involved in decision making related to work organisation.

In both transplant and harvest, labour is directly reciprocated. If Somboon and his wife work two labour days on the fields of Boonpop, four days on the fields of Taweechai, six days on Prachuap's land, and so on, they expect Boonpop to work two labour days on their land in return, Taweechai to reciprocate with four days, Prachuap with six days and so on.

While nobody counts precise hours and minutes or very consciously evaluates the performance of individual group members, rice farmers have rather good memories when it comes to reciprocation of labour. Conflict related to labour exchange is very rare: if a man does not contribute the time he should to the group effort, he might not be included in future group activities. For a Thai, such exclusion would make life economically very difficult since he would almost certainly have to try to hire workers from outside at a time when everybody is busy in their, or their neighbours', fields. Perhaps more importantly it would destroy his social life, which is based even more closely than the economy on eventual reciprocity of physical or financial input. Thus, there are sound economic and social reasons for individual submission to group solidarity and suppression of any inclination towards conflict with in-group members.

Relatives, friends and neighbours in a Thai rice-producing village have a very clear economic base to their social relations. This should not be taken as evidence of economic determinism. It can as easily be argued that the form cooperation takes is *socially* determined. If cooperation between ten adults would be sufficient to secure mutual economic benefits, none of the ten would object if the group expanded to twelve or fifteen or more members. The additional members after ten might bring no additional economic advantages, and might complicate the process of reciprocity, but they would be welcome as long as they form part of the larger social grouping within which economic activity takes place.

In practice it is quite usual for cooperation groups to contain too many participants rather than too few. Nobody wants to be left out. At the same time, groups usually remain of a self-manageable size in which all participants can sit down together, talk things over and eat together. Few groups contain less than ten people, few more than twenty.

Cooperative labour exchange involves the host family feeding all of the work party before and after work. Roles are reversed as hosts change from day to day. Thus the economic and the social are very much interrelated. This is perhaps why Thais use a single word – *ngan* – to mean both work and party.

Whatever else is carried over from village to town, the habit of distributing food on a rotational basis is retained. It maintains the link between work and social life. Even the most modern of workplaces in Thailand has regular and almost ritualistic circulations of things to munch. Nobody calculates but reciprocity takes place every bit as much in the office or on the shop floor as it does in the village. Reciprocal treating will occur almost daily within a small work group and less frequently on an enterprise wide basis. At the whole enterprise level of treating, you get a full chance to participate. Just like the village headman.

And now, to get an idea of how traditional aspects of Thai personality and behaviour might assist you, the urban headman, please refer to the next section, WORK GROUPS.

# WORK GROUPS

By knowingly allowing work groups to form when appropriate, and by forming individuals into units with group responsibility for goal achievement, you could save yourself a lot of time and effort and have a happier workforce doing a better job. You would also be making full use of existing traditional patterns of work organisation and complementing, rather than contradicting, Thai personality and preferences.

A drive through the countryside at the beginning of the rainy season in May-June will show many groups of people hard at work transplanting seedlings. The same drive at harvest time in November-December will show similar groups of a dozen or more adults working together. They work on land which, although owned or rented on a family basis, is worked cooperatively at important stages in the rice cycle.

Fine, but what has this to do with your urban workplace? Your people are busy with goods and services, sales, accounts, import-export, public relations and many other things. But not one person is engaged in rice cultivation. So, what lessons, if any, can be taken from traditional rural life and transplanted to the modern workplace?

The paradigm of a man engaged in ploughing

demonstrates clearly enough that when it is necessary to work alone, a motivated Thai can do so (see the preceding section, WORK AND RICE). But ploughing is an activity limited in time and balanced by more social work activities; nobody wants to spend his whole life walking alone behind a buffalo. So spare more than one thought for the motivation and happiness of the single chap alone in the dust-free computer room. If you want him to stay with you, a bit more social life than that provided by his high-tech buffalo might be in order.

If your secretary, who doesn't know one end of a buffalo from the other, finds it natural to cooperate with other staff members on some work activities, it would seem to make sense to allow such spontaneous self-organisation to flourish unless it contradicts the work goals that you are there to accomplish. By knowingly allowing work groups to form when appropriate, you could save yourself a lot of time and effort and have a happier workforce doing a better job.

The great majority of Thais are happiest, and usually most productive, when working in some form of group. The work group concept of management might have a few drawbacks for the manager who believes in individual performance evaluation; Thais merge in the group rather than demonstrate individual initiatives. But if work groups tend to stifle ambitious urges to outshine one's workmates, they also promote group responsibility and motivate the individual to perform at a rate equal to other members of the group. By letting up on the individual initiative and individual responsibility idea, you get consistency, teamwork and natural leadership.

If group organisation is appropriate for your activities, or at least for some of them, why not take things one step further? Foster a work environment not so very different from the rice fields by allowing and encouraging people to organise day-to-day work schedules within their group and by making groups rather than individuals the units responsible for reaching goals. The chances are that small groups will organise themselves and motivate their members much better than you could do. Which should leave you with more time to think about brightening up the life and performance of those doing jobs which do not fit group style organisation. You should also have more time to monitor goal achievement.

When the chips are down, you will be judged by your bosses or receive your profits according to how near you come to meeting your objectives. These objectives are the manager's ultimate reason for being. In pursuing them, you have nothing to fear and everything to gain by accommodating whenever possible and appropriate the preferences of your Thai work force for group patterns of work organisation. If you can do so, you will overcome any contradictions between the profit motive, happiness and personal ambition. Everybody gains.

# XENOPHOBIA

WE'RE THAIS
WE HAVE OUR KING
WE'VE NEVER BEEN
COLONISED.....
WELCOME TO
THAILAND

FARANG!

Almost all Thais are prepared to like you if given half a chance. Give them a whole chance. It makes life pleasant and is good for business.

The X slot stared blankly for a long time. Faced with the alternatives of xerox, Xhosa, Xmas, X-ray and xylophone, I finally plumped for xenophobia, a strong dislike or distrust of foreigners. Not that xenophobia exists to any noticeable degree in Thailand. But, with apologies to any Xhosa readers, this fact in itself makes the subject more relevant than any of the alternatives.

It is extremely difficult for an expat manager to motivate

a staff who have a strong dislike for foreigners. It is also extremely risky for the businessman to enter into agreements with people who cannot reach the first base of business, mutual trust. Fortunately, in Thailand, the expat manager or businessman is not likely to have much of a problem on this score. Now, that was worth knowing, wasn't it?

It remains possible, even in the centre of Bangkok, to find a young girl, perhaps fresh from upcountry or perhaps city born and bred, who is simply struck dumb at the very prospect of attempting to speak to a foreigner. She does not hate the foreigner, or fear him or distrust him. She just does not know how to fit him into the Thai system, which is the only one she knows. Although Bangkok is now a cosmopolitan city, not every Thai within it is cosmopolitan.

Thais who dislike foreigners do exist but they are remarkable as exceptions. Even this dislike rarely approaches anything like racism. This would seem to be indicated by the nature of ethnic jokes, which include the funny results of foreigners mispronouncing Thai words but are never based on long noses, skin colour, size of sexual organs and other obvious characteristics which distinguish racial types and are considered reasonable daily fare for cheap laughs in the West.

Far from being victims of racism, foreigners can expect to meet with a genuinely pleasant response from the great majority of Thais. Perhaps the days when foreigners had a scarcity value and were fawned over are gone forever, but the alien coming to work in Thailand today will still enjoy a reasonable amount of respect: certainly much more than a Thai expat worker can hope for outside Thailand.

Simply being white, black, Arab or Japanese does not earn you a high place on the status hierarchy, but it also does not relegate you to a low position or prevent you making your place within it, if that is your wish. All in all, most foreigners who live and work some time in Thailand appreciate the tolerant goodwill of the Thai people and are willing to admit that the world has a lot to learn from them.

# YEARS

Very often you will be faced with the need to translate the Buddhist Era year, normally used in Thailand, into the familiar Western equivalent. Remember the simple code 543 and subtract this figure from the Thai Buddhist year to find the Gregorian. Add 543 when calculating from Western to Thai.

A constant problem, even for those Thais who speak good English and those foreigners who speak good Thai, is knowing what year it is. Very basic, but this simple cultural difference in recording time has resulted in some expensive misunderstandings. If you are projecting returns in five years time and your Thai listener or reader understands three years, the potential for confusion is obvious.

To limit confusion, it is always best, when clearly making a statement from the present time, to say "in five years time" or "last year" or "seven years ago" rather than state the year. Then the listener will automatically make mental reference to his own calendar.

Fortunately for the expat manager, the Thai Buddhist year now begins and ends at the same time as the Gregorian calendar. Do not be confused that Thai New Year falls on 13-15 April!

Subcontinental businessmen familiar with the Buddhist calendar should pay particular attention to the fact that the *Thai* Buddhist calendar is one year behind that of Burma, India and Sri Lanka.

Reports and publications printed in Thailand, although written in English, very often carry only the Buddhist Era (B.E.) date. To find out the Western calendar equivalent subtract 543 years.

# ZZZ

Think carefully before introducing something which might not be needed or wanted.

The Thai alphabet, for all its forty four consonants, has no equivalent of the English Z sound. Never mind. It gets by perfectly well without it. Nobody in his right mind is going to suggest it should be introduced.

Not quite so obvious to many business managers, who will almost certainly have attended at least one course on supposedly international principles of business and management or at least have flicked through a few books on the genre before coming to Thailand, is that Thai society does not need a cultural Z imposed upon it. It can get by perfectly well without it.

Thus. If whatever management principle or practicality you want to use does not already exist in the Thai social context, it could well be a Z. Look around and consult your comprador to see if there is a Thai cultural equivalent that could do the job as well if not better. If there is not, think carefully before introducing something which might not be needed or wanted. If you can work with and through the Thai system, with small adaptations to fit you in, do it. It will almost certainly be cheaper, less disruptive, more effective and more profitable. Here endeth the lazt lezzon.

# THE AUTHOR

Robert Cooper, Ph.D. has lived outside of his native England most of his life. He is best known for the widely read *Culture Shock Thailand*, which he wrote together with his Thai wife, Nanthapa, and his books on the Hmong tribal minority in Northern Thailand, *Resource Scarcity and the Hmong Response* (Singapore University Press, 1984) and *The Hmong* (Tamarind Press, 1991). Since 1980, Robert has served in management positions with the United Nations in Thailand and overseas. He now lives in northern Thailand.

# INDEX